Well written, engaging, and completely accessible as an autobiography and a spiritual adventure. Love the parables and poems! We're seeing more awakening stories springing up among us regular people—herald of shifts to come, I suspect. Thank you for going public. I've personally been recommending the book to friends and colleagues. We wish you continued Magic Something!

—Leslie France, The Monroe Institute

In the lineage of Robert Pirsig's *Zen and the Art of Motorcycle Maintenance*, Carlos Castenada's Don Juan series, and William Least Heat-Moon's *Blue Highways,* Jeff Dixon's *21 Days* is a first-person account of a person's spiritual odyssey. Yet it is not the story of the journey up to the peak of the mountain, nor a reflection on what life looks like within that transcending nothingness. Instead, *21 Days* is a glimpse of what it looks like when you've come down the other side and returned to the world.

Dixon is no cardboard saint, nor does the life he reveals to us look all that much different from our own. If anything, perhaps he comes across as "more ordinary." And that's part of the magic of this book. The lessons he offers—lessons he's obviously learned himself—come not from "on high" but from right next door. And because they come from someone who looks at least as ordinary as we do, there is a promise that the truths we're reading about can really be learned and put into practice in our own lives. And when the "spiritual perfection" that is promised is that of a person who is sometimes annoyed by his child, frustrated by his partner, and bored by his job, then those moments when the "magic something" is flowing seem simultaneously all the more miraculous and all the more attainable. This is quite a feat, and *21 Days* is quite a book.

—Erik Walker Wikstrom, Unitarian Universalist minister and author of *Simply Pray: A Modern Prayer Practice to Deepen Your Life*

I read with delight Jeff Stewart Dixon's *21 Days*. I knew Jeff in the days when he was searching, unhappy, having glimpses, then feeling he "lost it." Reading this book I could feel a true and authentic shift in him indicative of a realization and embodied awakening that is no longer felt to come and go.

Although on the surface it is a simple and accessible text set in everyday language, without spiritual jargon and nondual double speak, don't let this simplicity fool you. A rich tapestry of parables, stories, and insights envelop the reader with deep wisdom in navigating the terrain of finding that "magic something." Additionally, there is a transmission found in his description of living every day with this "magic something" that orients the reader to its living possibility.

—Solané Verraine, Satsang teacher,
student of Eli Jaxon Bear and Gangaji

21

days

a guide for spiritual beginners

J. Stewart Dixon

PIE
publishing

Cover design by Darren Wheeling (www.blackegg.com)
Cover art by Photos.com
Interior design by Jane Hagaman

If you are unable to order this book from your local bookseller, you
may order directly from the publisher's website.

www.spiritualityforbadasses.com

Production services provided by Quartet Books
www.quartetbooks.com

Library of Congress Control Number: 2012913607

ISBN 978-0-9858579-3-6
10 9 8 7 6 5 4 3 2 1
Printed on acid-free paper in the United States

2021 Forward

It's been over ten years now since I wrote this book! I still like it. I'm still proud of it. That's sayin' something– many authors become critical or embarrassed of their own work over time. Not here. Maybe I'd change a word or sentence or two, (I didn't) but for the most part, I still dig 21 Days. I feel it was accurate, honest and clear when I wrote it. I feel the same about it today. Enjoy...

Spiritual growth, insight and awakening doesn't have to be complicated. 21 Days is a journal / memoir (and excellent guide for you) of the first twenty-one days of spiritual awakening and discovery that happened to me in 2010. I had been seeking in earnest with western American advaita nondual, nonduality teachers like Eckhart Tolle, Gangaji, Adi Da, Adyashanti, Saniel Bonder, Andrew Cohen (and more) for about 10 years.

This book chronicles the first 21 days of this awakening in all its ordinariness and extra-ordinariness. I like spiritual parables (ala Paula Coehlo or Richard Bach) so there are quite a few in this book as well.

Lastly, 21 Days was written with beginners in mind so I didn't use the typical flowery, obtuse, nondual spiritual language. I'm a blue collar / engineer type of guy, married and live in the suburbs of Virginia- so I wrote it from this point of view.

Peace & Laughter,
J Stewart / Author:
21 Days: A Guide for Spiritual Beginners
Spirituality for Badasses: How to find inner peace and happiness without losing your cool

Contents

Introduction

Eventually, so it seems, most of us at some point or another turn off that forlorn, neglected little switch called magic and turn away, oblivious to our heavy hearts, and plod off into the misadventure called adulthood. Yet hauntingly built into the fabric of our being from the moment of birth, *magic* seemed naturally destined to grow and blossom into *something*.

In some cases, in a few of us, this switch never gets completely turned off. It instead is lost or buried in life's chaos, only surfacing here and there for brief moments. For many people, Christmas is perhaps the last vestige of this switch. One day each year, Christmas casts a soft warm blanket of this promised *something* over and amidst our little globe, temporarily softening heavy hearts and eliciting a better world and a better you. As adults, across most cultures, we seem to limit our experience of this *magic something*—call it happiness, contentment, fulfillment, or, alternatively, awakening, enlightenment, or the peace that passeth all understanding—to just one or a few special days each year. Too bad.

So what would it be like if you lived *every day* as if it were a special day? What if, along with the intelligence and responsibility of an adult, you could sustain the happy innocence of a child, accompanied by an extraordinary feeling of bodily peace and mental contentment? And what if, just as a trial period, you actually lived this way *without effort,* for twenty-one consecutive days?

I did. What is recounted in this book is not a work of fiction. I don't do drugs. I'm not an Indian mystic. I don't live in a monastery. I don't have a brain tumor. I'm not a member or advocate of some new-age positive-thinking cult. I'm not a religious zealot. I'm pretty much like you: married, kid, dog, two cats, job, and mortgage. I'm forty-one.

I have been prone to these sustained experiences of *magic something* for about six years now.

I am acquainted with many other people who have had these experiences. I am acquainted with people who live in this state permanently. My case is not a fluke. *How* I arrived to live with this *magic something* is of course an obvious question, and while I do address this, it is not the main focus of this book. Reading about this state—that it did, does, and can happen—is the primary focus of *21 Days.*

I've tried to describe these experiences in a very plain and simple fashion, without technical, religious, spiritual, or psychological jargon; hopefully creating a book that is both friendly and comprehensible—one you'd happily lend to a friend without hesitation or fear of embarrassment.

Whether you think this is a work of fiction or not is, I suppose, dependent upon the distance you have traveled from your own childhood *magic something* switch. Is it still there? I'm guessing you're about to find out.

I say with hard-earned confidence, birthed from time, diligence, and repeated experience: I have turned my *magic some-*

thing switch on. Follow me: The door is open, and you are welcome to come right in. May *21 Days* inspire you and challenge you. And, if you are a weary soul like I was, may *21 Days* serve to help and heal you.

Peace and Laughter,
Jeff Stewart Dixon

Ice-Cream Cone

Life is worth one lick if you have shelter.

Life is worth two licks if you have shelter and money.

Life is worth three licks if you have shelter, money, and friends.

Life is worth four licks if you have shelter, money, friends, and a loving family.

Life is worth five licks if you have shelter, money, friends, a loving family, and good health.

Life is worth six licks if you have shelter, money, friends, a loving family, good health, and god.

Life is worth seven licks if you have shelter, money, friends, a loving family, good health, god, and a humble heart.

Life is worth eight licks if you have shelter, money, friends, a loving family, good health, god, a humble heart, and a divine purpose.

Life is worth nine licks if you have shelter, money, friends, a loving family, good health, god, a humble heart, a divine purpose, and divine fulfillment.

Life is worth ten licks if you have shelter, money, friends, a loving family, good health, god, a humble heart, a divine purpose, divine fulfillment, and a religion named after you.

Life is worth the whole damn ice-cream cone if you're just simply . . . happy.

I seem to be getting up at an ungodly hour as of late: four o'clock, five thirty, six thirty, seven o'clock if I'm lucky. One reason, I wager, is due to the fact that I have a three-year-old son. Anyone who has a baby or toddler or little tyke can painfully tell you about the long-ago demise of Olympic sleeping. Maybe that's why today I'm up at five a.m., or maybe I'm just excited. For five days now I've been living in La-la Land, and I'm lying in bed pondering the situation.

One of the immediate effects of waking up with the feeling of permanent Christmas is the endless set of possibilities that lie before you. Usually my first thoughts in the morning are more oriented around obstacles, stress, a long day's work, and getting my hands on a strong cup of chemically induced false sense of enthusiasm—I love coffee. But today, at this wee hour, I am stewing in a swirl of possibility, creativity, and emptiness. In other words, I'm a blank canvas, and like an excited kid with a pack of crayons, I wanna get busy.

This particular motivation is due part and parcel to the fact that I have always been in one way or another a creative type. I paint. I write both words and music. I'm an amateur woodworker. In general, I like designing, building, implementing, and completing things, with no set of instructions to burden me. To a certain degree, I even do this for a living. So it is on this morning that I have come up with one creative gem of an idea, and it has me lying awake at five in the morning: Write down for twenty-one days what it's like, as a forty-one-year-old adult male, to return to a feeling that is basically akin to Christmas, Oz, Never Land, and Shangri-La all rolled into one.

What it actually feels like is this: From my head to my toes, for good stretches of the day, I am pervaded by a sense of peace, equanimity, and contentment that has no experiential match. I just call it *magic something*.

In detail, a typical *magic something* episode feels like this. It begins with a strong sense of feeling returning to my arms, hands, legs, and feet; then quickly transforms into a deep, warm, soft, full body awareness. Simultaneously, the faculties that govern agility, dexterity, and overall bodily control refine themselves and expand. I become infused with a very palpable, athletic, cat-like, and animal sense of physicality. My posture straightens out. I hold my head high. My chest naturally protrudes upward and outward. I breathe deeply. Visually, my perception expands, and I begin to perceive through what seems to be the outer surfaces of my eyeballs. Everything I see is clearer and brighter. My eyes are wide open. I feel an increased blood flow through the veins of my neck. I sense a subtle and pleasurable pressure in both hemispheres of my brain. I begin to believe that anything and everything can happen, and it will *all* be good. When I walk, there is a nimbleness to my stride; I feel as if I am gliding or floating. My heart twinges with delight, and I transform into a ridiculously giddy—and innocent—little schoolboy. I could do cartwheels in the fields of the universe. I am happy with a capital H. I banter with people. I am eager to help. I am approachable and warm. I smile easily and laugh at the drop of a hat. This . . . is *magic something* . . . as I know it, and as I live it.

It took me most of my adult life to arrive here. It was no accident. I intentionally sought this state. It took about seventeen years of earnest seeking before I had my first good glimpse, then another five or six years of integration and repetition to really understand it. Yes, it's a long-term investment, but the payoff is worth every penny. Since the initial glimpse, I've spent countless hours, days, and months living with this *magic something*. There are permanent benefits as well: *Magic something* introduced a type of healing that no modern medicine can deliver—a permanent sense of well-being and peace of mind.

I'm excited. Let me tell you why. *Magic something* is a pretty damn good feeling, and sooner or later, if you're having this kind of experience, you're gonna wanna tell somebody about it. I play around with this writing idea, go over it in my mind, view it from all sorts of angles, and basically work myself into a tizzy, as if I were playing catch with a freshly dug-up twenty-million-dollar diamond. I do this a lot. Inception is one of the parts of creativity I love best. Artistic follow through, as evidenced by the book in your hands, is the part I revel in.

My three-year-old son meanders sleepy-eyed into the room, gently interrupting and concluding my silent reverie. Time to get up and hitch myself to the unfolding of the day. I say *unfolding*, because that's what it feels like: There is nothing of real urgency I need to do, make happen, or guide. I am out of the picture, and the day simply unfolds. And even better, I am confident it will unfold in a pretty okay fashion, in alignment with just about everything: from my left dirty sock to the ache in my lower back to the recently discovered quasar on the far side of the Milky Way galaxy. There's nothing I really need to do. I relinquish all control. That's my outlook at six in the morning. Not a bad start.

"Papa, I wanna go downsteers."

Jeremy plops himself onto my bed and begins tugging at my shirt sleeve. He stands. I take cover. He jumps on my face. Okay. Face jumping always works. I oblige.

My morning routine is pretty typical of those that are dictated by a three-year-old, two cats, a pit bull, and an overwhelming urge to caffeinate. Jeremy likes to be picked up at this juncture, so I perform a one-handed service to all those in need: Water goes on to boil; Lilly (the pit bull) goes outside on the lead; Rusty and Gypsy lumber after us down to the basement where they get dry crap dumped into their bowls. I walk back upstairs. Lilly comes back inside. Jeremy is set down. Water finishes boiling. Coffee gets French pressed. I take two sips. Jeremy dips his finger in the coffee. I relax for five seconds, and the routine is then hijacked by a three-year-old's whims: Read a book, eat breakfast, ride my neck, inspect and pick the days' crop of morning glories, make a playdough mess, and/or—the mack daddy of all morning enterprises—zoom around in the house at high speed in the baby stroller to the rhythm of bluegrass music blaring from the radio. Daddy pushes. Lilly chases. Did I mention that Mama is still sleeping upstairs in bed? I don't know how she does it.

All of this is done in the space of normal love, acceptance, and quasi-boredom. It's a routine. I happily engage in it, but I am an intelligent human being. There are only so many times one can feed the cats before going into brain-off automaton mode. I do, however, most of the time, get a kick out of bluegrass stroller derby.

The quality and quantity of *magic something* imbuing me at this hour is light and subtle. I feel pretty ordinary. In short, I am pleasantly relieved of being the usual grump I can be at this time of day. For whatever reason, on most days, the fireworks don't start until a little later. It's eight o'clock now, and Mama is getting out of bed. Jeremy hears her and scampers upstairs to join her in *her* routine. I finish my breakfast, then begin preparing for the day.

I'm self-employed and have been since I was twenty-four. I own an audio/video company that sells and installs home theaters, church sound systems, office projectors, etc. I do this work from the basement of our home. I spend about half my days in the office working up quotes and designing systems and the other half out in the field installing. When I need help, I have a couple of subcontract guys. I have a van that hauls around my tools and supplies. It's a basic scheme. It pays the bills. Occasionally, I win a contract that does more than pay the bills. I work nine to five. I don't work weekends. I have plenty of time for family, fishing, and pondering the nature of life.

I gather together my backpack and prepare to leave. I have a consultation meeting at nine a.m. It's with a couple who just moved into town who wish to renovate their house audio/video. All I really need is pen and paper, but I strap a tape measure to my belt for . . . uh . . . good measure—and some extra flair. By the way, if you haven't seen the movie *Office Space*, you should. It's a great flick about a guy who accidentally has his *magic something* switch turned on.

I say goodbye to Elisabeth and Jeremy. As I head out the door, *my switch* goes into overdrive. There must be something about human interaction that causes it to blossom. It's a little unnerving, slightly disorienting, and fairly pleasurable. *Magic something* pervades my entire body. My eyes are wide open. I am happy.

My customer lives about fifteen minutes away. I arrive and park on the street outside the house. I am having a slight problem. The euphoria is so strong I can barely focus. It takes me a few stumbling minutes to gather everything I need, which is not much, but in this state might as well be the tools required to scuba dive the Marianas Trench.

I walk toward the door, hoping my pants are still on, and knock. The customer answers, welcomes me in, and we get down to business. I won't bore you with the details of our conversation, but I can tell you that my consultation was about as focused as a bumblebee in a hurricane. Every option seems feasible to me. A fifty-foot television mounted to the roof? Sure! This is one of the pleasant hazards of this strange orientation. Nothing seems impossible. Everything is ultimately okay. We walk from room to room, and despite the circumstances, I am able to give this person my uncompromised attention.

Let me confess that I don't find this work terribly challenging or the topic very interesting anymore. I've installed hundreds and hundreds of televisions, and at this point, I can do it blindfolded, upside-down, and with a straitjacket on. Usually, of course, I rise above this boredom in the name of making a buck, but there is no need of that today, because I am lost in the bosom of this insanely unreasonable happiness. In the end, I gather my focus and we come up with a plan which serves as a template for the quote and design. I say goodbye, make my way to the car, and head back home.

I should mention eye contact. While with this customer, I sustained near-perfect eye contact the entire time. I didn't do this because I was trying to do this. It is just a natural by-product of the *magic something* state. When you have everything you're ever going to want right in the moment, you have nothing to lose or hide or cover up, and open-eyed honesty just naturally arises. There is no agenda and no fear. This may sound pedantic, but trust me, it's *not.* Human interaction on this level is an astounding element of living with *magic something.* The cherry on top is that it's like this with just about everyone.

I arrive home and do a little office work. Not being particularly motivated by this work, I head upstairs and volunteer my time with Jeremy. Elisabeth is a stay-at-home mom, so her day job is child care for Jeremy. Professionally she's a seamstress but generally has very little of that work to do these days. Today, however, she does have some work, so I take acorn duty.

In our front yard we have a large decorative bed of gravel, strewn with acorns from the adjacent oak tree. This is where Jeremy rules supreme with his buckets and diggers. Today we are making his favorite dish: rock and acorn soup. Having concocted this soup with him about three hundred and forty-two other times, it's a little tedious, but it's a nice day, and I'm still grooving on the *magic something* euphoria, so it's all good. I deeply relax and allow myself to melt unburdened into the circumstance of the moment. It's Christmas. I'm opening presents. In this state, I am in *much* better tune with my body. There is full feeling awareness throughout. I breathe in big heavy truckloads of air.

"Papa, you put the acorns in dare. I dig dem with dis digger. Scoop."

"'Like this?"

"Yep, you do it. Like dat."

A few hours pass and Elisabeth finishes her work. I break for lunch, then attend to the next very important part of the day: fishin'. We live on a lake and I love to fish; fly-fishing especially, but I have no problem swinging big clunky lures from a bait casting reel, hoping to catch big clunky bass. I grab my bait casting getup and head down to our pier. I spend twenty-five blissful moments entertaining myself this way. Three bass join in the fun. I thank the powers that be for this fine Christmas Day moment and head back up to the house to check emails and phone messages. Nothing important here. I check in with Elisabeth again and resume daddy duty. Jeremy and I head out with his diggers and shovels in tow to the local playground and get busy there for a little while. We return and head into the evening portion of our day.

It's Friday. We often go out to eat as a family on Fridays. Today we decide to try a new Thai restaurant. Unfortunately, this decision is made about a half hour behind my stomach's schedule, and I skid into grumpy/hungry territory. I'm still in *magic something* mode, but when my body sends me a signal that something needs attending to—for example, eating, sleeping, drinking, peeing, etc.—I have to respond immediately or the alarm sounds causing agitation or irritation. Grumpy Papa, in other words. I'm starving by the time we get to the restaurant. We order, and a few minutes later, I wolf down a spring roll. The rest of the outing goes as planned. Good food. Good service. Elisabeth and I chat, and Jeremy bounces off the Asian-decorated walls, a pristine example of that rare creature aptly named "bull in a china shop."

We exit and embark upon the second to last adventure of the day: the grocery store. Having replenished my body's energy, I am back to feeling the *magic something* groove. As we enter the grocery store, the groove launches into hyperdrive. There are *a lot* of people in this grocery store. I am soon transported to the far side of Mars. Yet strangely, I am completely present here on Earth. Open eyed, I am attuned to everyone here in this humble store. Rich ones. Poor ones. Old ones. New ones. Large ones. Pretty ones. Ugly ones. Broken ones. Unhappy ones. Lost ones. Suffering ones. Okay ones. I see them all and my heart goes out. I want to share this Christmas day with them. I want to tell them that *there is* an ocean. *There is* more to life than this desert. I have seen it, swum in it. I know others who have done the same. I want to shout this gospel from the top of the cereal aisle. I simply want to share the joy.

Instead, choosing not to make an ass of myself, I head over to the produce aisle and grab an avocado. Oh well. We pay for our groceries, exit, and make our way home.

It's time for bed now. My superpowers are winding down to just a background hum. Elisabeth is putting the groceries away, and Jeremy is confining his bouncing to the upstairs walls. I give him a bath. We do some variation of wrestling, reading, playing with Legos, etc., then Mama comes up and puts him to sleep. I'm tired. Energy seems to burn more efficiently in this state. When the tank's empty, it's empty. It's probably around nine p.m. now. I lumber into the bedroom. Read a bit. Lights out.

The Feather

Once upon a time, a feather dropped down from the sky. It had fallen from the right wing of a Yellow-Rumped Warbler.

The warbler had miscalculated a swoop between the branch of a small conifer and a cerulean blue balloon, which had lodged itself in the tree the previous day after five-year-old Joshua had accidentally released it while strolling in the park with his mother. The bird struck the branch, consequently dislodging the feather.

Before the feather hit the ground, Bella, John's Chesapeake Labrador retriever, caught a glimpse of it, jerked her leash out of John's hand, and took off after it. Bella's leash crossed paths with Jim, who was jogging on the nearby footpath. Jim tripped over the leash and stumbled into Henry. Henry was making his routine walk to work with his red plastic mug of coffee in one hand and black briefcase in the other. The coffee splashed and several large mocha colored droplets landed on a newspaper. The newspaper belonged to Jennifer, who was seated on a bench waiting for the bus.

Jennifer is divorced, and has two kids she raises on her own. She's a waitress at Sal's diner across town. Just before the coffee hit her paper, she had wished (a big wish) for something more in her life.

No longer able to read the headline news, she turned to the employment section and saw an advertisement for a night school offering degrees in the health industry. She liked what she read. She kept on reading. Three days later she applied. Three years later, she received a degree, quit her job at Sal's, and found employment as a physical therapist's assistant. That same year, she met a man, Gabriel, who courted her and later asked her to marry him. She said yes.

The years went by. She became a physical therapist. Her children went on to college. Life with Gabriel was pretty good. One day, feeling restless, she went for a walk and meandered by the old park bench she used sit on while waiting for the cross-town bus to Sal's. She couldn't put her finger on it— despite the fact that her life was very good now, *something* was still wrong. Something was still missing from her life, and she wished (a big wish) she knew why.

It was just in that moment . . . that a feather dropped down from the sky.

It's Saturday, seven a.m. I'm having a rare Jeremy-free morning. He and Mama are still sleeping upstairs. Cats and dog are fed. I have a cup of coffee in my hand. I'm walking down to our pier, not to fish but to take in the mist rising off the lake. The view is storybook beautiful. I plop myself down on old planks of wood. I've brought my camera but not to photograph the lake. There's something else down here which has also caught my attention: a hot air balloon on the horizon. Two in fact. They make huge, powerful whooshes as hot air is force bellowed into their balloons. It's an inspiring collage of sight and sound. Not a bad way to begin the day. I take a few bad photographs then sit and watch strings of white fog vaporize off the glassy lake. I meander back to the house. I've got the double kung-fu whammy morning delight going on now: *magic something* and caffeine. Yes, I'm a happy junkie.

Right about this time Elisabeth and Jeremy clunk downstairs, and we all eat breakfast together. Today I've got extended babysitting duty so Elisabeth can do some sewing, which means papa and son are goin' on an adventure. Oddly enough, I'm really having a hard time deciding what to do, so I give up my efforts and allow the universe to decide. Before leaving, I hop into the shower. Got it! The zoo! Perfect. Not far away. Enough thrills to occupy a few hours and, more importantly, enough thrills to occupy a three-year-old's brain. It's a local barnyard petting zoo with a few exotics thrown in. Not much, but quaint, and cheap. I shower, get dressed, and fly downstairs. I tell Jeremy, and he's beside himself with joy. Great. That makes two of us. The deal is clinched. We begin packing the requisite stuff: water, camera, shoes, sunglasses, veggie sticks, cash, etc. Hugs are made. We say bye-bye to Mama.

"Papa, we go onna venture? To the zoooo?"

"Yep, we're going to the zoo dude."

"Papa, you see a bearrr?"

"Yep, I saw a bear."

"We goin' to da zoooo, Papa?"

"Yep, we sure are, man."

It's a perfectly clear and mild October day. It's a nice drive. We're headed into the mountains and the trees are just beginning to display their burnt umber and gold tourist-attracting colors. I'm enamored. The cumulus clouds dangling in the blue sky are a nice touch also. I'm now sinking into the feeling of doing nothing at all and utterly enjoying it. Jeremy's chattering away in the backseat about the types of animals we'll see. Together we trump any bourgeoisie safari to Africa.

We arrive and enter through the small gate. Time to get jiggity with the animals. We are handed a big bowl of feed. Mr. Camel is our first meet and greet. He is happy to see us. I plop down cross-legged on the ground to be face to face with Jeremy and Mr. Camel. It's a good time. The camel eagerly takes our feed. He's soft and fuzzy. Jeremy is wary of getting too close. I understand. From this angle the camel might as well be a dinosaur. A few ponies join us. Some other kids and their parents come around.

I am the only adult sitting on the ground, and I am lost in the happy frenzy of little people, Mr. Camel, and ponies. To me, all this seems normal and the right action, but I can tell that the other adults are wondering why I am wallowing in the dirt.

Here's the thing: I probably have more in common with the contentment of the kids and the animals than I do with the reserved stuffiness of the grown-ups. In the *magic something* state, there are no rules or inhibitions or calculated maneuvers. Of course, I'm not going to rip my clothes off and dance naked on a picnic table, but I'm also not going to deny myself the simple pleasure of relaxing into the moment. This relaxation extends to my entire body, and so I have no compunction about dropping to the ground to be on eye level with everyone else. The dirt on the ground does not offend me. I am not disconnected from the animals or the kids. I'm swimming carefree in the midst of it all. It feels great.

The next meet and greet is with Mr. Brown Calf. He's adorable, completely lovable, and comes adorned with a very cool brass cowbell. He's irresistible. Jeremy and I fawn all over him. He's our favorite of the day. Who'd a thought you could fall for a cow? We meet and greet the rest of the animals: turkeys, pig, ducks, donkeys, goats, and an albino wallaby. Everyone eagerly accepts our handfuls of feed. We amble around the small enclosure, feeling the warm waning October sun on our skin. The

Blue Ridge Mountains loom in the background, chaperoning the entire occasion. I breath deeply, walk slowly, gracefully. I'm in the flow of a day imbued with a circus-like atmosphere of happiness and warmth.

We express our thanks to the owners and leave. Jeremy is tired, and I'm hungry. There's a pizza place a few miles down the road. We pull in, grab some food, and are on our way. In a few short minutes, Jeremy falls asleep in the backseat. I settle in for the drive home, anchored to the moment and to the rock and earth below us. I'm feeling as rooted as those ancient mountains in front of me.

We arrive home. Mama takes Jeremy upstairs to bed. I've now got some free papa time, so I head down to the pier to fish. I make a few casts here and there, but nobody wants to play. Oh well. I walk back up to my office and, even though it's Saturday, check my emails. There's one that's got my attention. Nothing to do with business.

This email is a direct result of my comically ambitious, anything is possible, *magic something* state. It's a reply to an inquiry I sent out a few days ago concerning a 4.5-million-dollar, five-hundred-acre property. Yep, I'm deluded. I've always dreamed of owning my own big farm, but right now I think I have about 4.5 dollars I could put down on a property this size. It's a ridiculous notion. No harm in sending out the email I guess. Turns out this property was owned by the former saxophone player for the Dave Matthews Band. He passed away last year in an ATV accident. A pointless and sad death. Whoever owns the farm now wants to liquidate it. But we're in the middle of a recession, and I bet there aren't too many people willing to plop down that kind of dough on a residence. Maybe I could set it up as

a nature retreat center? Rent it on the weekends? Camp there?
Okay . . . fish there? I dunno. I send the real estate agent a return
email asking him to call me on Monday. I'm a deluded fool. But
a happy one.

Jeremy the post-nap crank is up, and Elisabeth and I are preparing for the next event of the day. We are having some friends
and their two children (two and five) over for dinner. They're
due to arrive around five p.m. Elisabeth is cooking. I'm cleaning and watching the crank. A knock is heard at the door and
the evening begins. Jeremy perks up. We talk. Drink some wine.
Eat dinner. The kids play down near the freeway (kidding). It's a
nice evening—good company and a welcome change from our
nightly routine. The wine doesn't affect my groove much, just
makes it sloppy.

Speaking of which, I'd prefer to avoid the whole alcohol and
magic something analogy, but most people have had a drink or
two, so I think it can serve to describe my experience. Here it
is: Indeed, living with *magic something* is a little like having a
light beer or wine buzz. Except there are no detrimental physical side effects. No loss of coordination. No speech impairment.
No numbing of the senses. It's a crappy comparison, but worth
mentioning.

Our guests leave. It's late. Jeremy's wired, but somehow Elisabeth wrangles him into bed. I'm downstairs attacking a mountain of dishes. Elisabeth comes downstairs after Jeremy falls
asleep. She's on the computer. I say goodnight with a kiss. I stroll
upstairs. Brush my teeth. Get undressed. Lights out.

Secret Church

Have you heard about the secret church? I discovered it about two months ago. The pastor is a very dynamic and engaging individual, but a little radical, so the church keeps a low profile. Most of the time, about twenty to thirty people show up. Very nice people—working class, with jobs, families, and all the usual responsibilities. The church doesn't have a lot of money, so there's nothing fancy about the service or the surroundings. As a matter of fact, they don't even have a permanent facility yet, which is okay, because it would probably draw too much attention anyway—this church is not liked by the ruling authority around here. They claim the church teaches antigovernment and anti-authoritarian ideas. Too much emphasis on individual rights, freedom, and happiness. But I know better. Radical ideas. Different ideas. The truth. This is what scares them. So the church stays underground, and every week—it's a hassle—I follow a new trail of fish symbols marked on buildings, pointing the way to the meeting place. It's a good church. I'd like to keep going. I hope the pastor—Jesus, I heard his name was—can make a go of it. I sorta like the guy.

It's six thirty a.m. Jeremy's up early today, and he's tugging at my blankets, pressing me to go downstairs. I roll over. He amps it up a notch and begins crawling and bouncing on my face. Effective as usual. Awake now, I concede to his desires. We walk downstairs. The morning routine ensues, including bluegrass stroller derby. We add to it an excursion down to the pier where I show him the mist rising off the lake. He likes it. We return. It's about eight thirty. Elisabeth enters the scene, and we all have breakfast together. I have permission to go fly-fishing this morning, but I surprise her and tell her I'm going to church, not because I'm feeling particularly pious this morning, but because the effects of tropical storm Nicole are still muddying my usual fishing holes. In the end, however, I'm glad I do go to church.

Since moving to central Virginia three years ago, I still haven't found the right church: a place where I can be myself; a place I can love—for the people, the message, and the environment. Still haven't found it. This is why I'm feverishly Googling churches on the Internet at nine in the morning. I've been in about a dozen churches in our area, mostly because my work takes me there, so I'm familiar with most of the names that pop up in the search engine. There's one that catches my attention. It's called Sojourner's Church and, as coincidence would have it, is the church that Jeremy's school uses for public gatherings. He hasn't started school yet, but he's enrolled, and I get frequent emails from them about gatherings at this church. I decide to give it a try. As a backup plan, I take note that there are several other churches in the area.

I say goodbye and hop in the car. *Magic something* at this point has already ballooned out of control. A feeling of heightened sensitivity, solid physical ground, and timeless flow has permeated my body and mind. Except, there's just one hitch—I've also got a knot of stress in my stomach the size of a bowling ball. This is an odd, seemingly contradictory, sensation. I can only explain it this way: When I am in this state, the feeling of *magic something* is always primary. It's equivalent to being completely aware of the water at the *bottom* of the pool—temperature, currents, cleanliness, clarity, PH, etc. It's pretty stable. Simultaneously, I am privy to the usual litany of other states that appear on the surface of the pool: stress, anger, sadness, excitement, boredom, irritation, etc. These are experienced as small waves that come and go quickly. It's a bit schizophrenic but better than the alternative, which is to identify with the small waves all the time.

So, I've got a bowling alley in my stomach, because basically I am nervous about attending this new church, standing out, being noticed, etc. I'm also becoming deeply skeptical that I'm going to like this church. The situation is driving me nuts, but I persevere and arrive in the parking lot. It's full—a good sign, I guess. I park the car and nervously make my way to the front entrance. It's your basic white wood-framed steeple and brick church, circa the 1970s. There's an acre or so of grass—sparsely populated with trees—gravel, and crumbly sidewalk that surrounds the church. Not particularly fancy. Not shabby or run down either. Utilitarian is a good description. There's a parish hall, some offices, and maybe a nursery all attached to the main sanctuary. I don't see or enter any of these rooms, because as I pass through the main doors, I land right where I should be: in the narthex, two steps and an open doorway away from the back of the sanctuary. There's a service going on. I'm late, miserably so—maybe the sixth or seventh inning. As I enter the sanctuary, I am a dizzying mixture of *magic something* and nervousness. It takes me about thirty seconds to realize that I probably should remove my baseball cap. I do so and lean against the rear wall corner to survey the lay of the land. I notice an empty seat to my left and decide in the name of calming my nerves to sit down. I do, and it's immediately better.

I allow the vibe of the church to enter my being. I breath deeply, and slowly I am relieved, because this is what I realize: This is a church for losers. And my heart, the engine room of *magic something*, immediately recognizes that it is okay here; that it can be itself here; that there is no need to hide here—because what my heart knows, above all other knowing, is that I too am a loser. I am not a winner. I am not triumphant. I am not king. I did not arrive at *magic something* by winning or succeeding or dominating. I came here by way of loss, by way of defeat. I am home. This is a good church.

The pastor is a woman, dignified, down to earth, in her mid-fifties. She is standing at ground level. There is no riser, no pulpit, no fancy wall or pedestal of stuff separating her from us. At her feet is a small wooden table. She is surrounded in semi-circle fashion by church members seated in single-cushioned seats. Laid out on the table beneath her are baskets containing an assortment of breads; fresh-baked breads, not those thin, bleached-white wafer things. She announces communion. Moments later she holds up the chalice. It's a real chalice, made from brown pottery and worn by years of use. There's no gold in this church. Above her head is a vaulted white ceiling lined with thick, dark, wooden beams. The PA system she is using is abysmal, delivering more feedback than sound. No one seems to mind. But my oversensitive audio-engineering ears keep tripping the breaker in my brain that imagines the two pieces of gear and three minutes it would take to fix it.

The communion process begins, and I take closer notice of the people: In general, a younger crowd. No sea of blue hair here. No affluence, mostly lower to middle class. White, black, and Hispanic. Straight and gay. There are several disabled people.

One of them stands out because he speaks in a loud, nasally, awkward fashion. There's an overweight gay female couple sitting in the row of seats directly in front of me. There's a straggly bearded mendicant-looking fellow standing in the far right aisle six or seven rows ahead of me. There's a good-looking younger couple with their two-year-old a few feet away. There's an older couple, who I'm guessing have seen the seasons change seventy or eighty times. There's a hoary old guy, who looks like a highway crewman, complete with dirty blue jeans and yellow leather work boots. There's another gay couple—male, balding, mid-fifties, tough looking, stout, and no-nonsense—on the left side of the room.

I notice all of these people. I notice their happiness, their pain, their strife and struggle; their long-haul march through life. There are nearly a hundred souls filling the seats in this church. I am a cloud of *magic something* Jell-o now.

The a cappella choir seated in the loft above my head begins singing an enchantingly beautiful song. The whole church joins in. There's no musical accompaniment, no super duper, sound-reinforced, mega PA system. It's simple and simply haunting. I fall further into reverie as the music plumbs the depths of my heart.

It's a song whose true melody is heard only by those in sympathy, by those willing to admit defeat, by those whose lonely feet have shuffled them into the only place they can go—onto this tiny lit island in a sea of darkness. A good church is a resting place where you can openly confess that it is simply hard just to *be here,* just to be struggling to survive, just to be breathing in the thin precious air. This is an important confession, because it is the first step on the path to full *magic something* recovery.

If only on this day and in this moment, the people here have heard this melody and have made this confession, then they are another step closer to finding their own *magic something*. Yes, this is a good church.

Communion is now over. The somber tone has been replaced by a cheerier one as the pastor announces that they will be introducing new church members. A wreath assembled from multi-colored ribbons is brought down from its resting place on the far right wall. New official members of the church are asked to come forward. They do so. There are about ten. A little something is said about each. As they are introduced, a new ribbon is added to the wreath.

It's a messy, bulky thing, the wreath. The pastor acknowledges its disheveled state, wryly commenting on its similarities to faith. In essence, she hits the nail on the head. Life is a messy mystery. I couldn't agree more.

After this ceremony, the service comes to a conclusion. Everyone in the church spreads to the periphery, joins hands, and a short prayer is spoken. The heart of the matter has been dealt with, so this part is done quickly and sweetly. The pastor gives a final blessing and the service ends. It's time to go. I'm not much for goodbyes or social lingering in instances like this, and because I also feel like I've just skydived off the space shuttle, I exit through the rear doors and make my way to the car.

On my way out, I am served a final slice of humble pie. There are two homeless people, a man and a woman, both in their fifties, sitting on the bench smoking cigarettes. Their presence startles me. Their iron facial expressions speak volumes. They are bereft, lost, suffering, bound to some untouchable limbo where escape seems impossible; where self-esteem is so low they do not even allow themselves the tiny luxury of actually *entering* the church. I am saddened by their condition, but as I walk by I realize—I am no saint. The brutal truth is that I am not qualified to help them. They are in need of help on a practical level. This mysterious *magic something* that has flooded my being is, in the end, a luxury. And while it resonates with sympathy, it does not dictate that I save the world. I am able to choose my own battles, and sometimes this means ignoring them in favor of fully concentrating on the larger war. Still, I am saddened, and I feel like a heartless stranger as I pass them by.

I walk to my car, thankful that I have chosen this church, and make a quick exit. The drive home is uneventful. I return to find Jeremy and Elisabeth out front playing rocks.

"Hey. How was your morning?" I say.

"Good. How was it?" asks Elisabeth.

"Fine. I went to a church called Sojourner's—"

"Papa . . ."

"Heard of it?

"No."

"The church Waldorf school uses for meetings—"

"Papa, you go fishing?"

"No buddy, I went to church. A place where there's lots of people."

"You not go fishing?"

"Not today, Munchkin." I turn to Elisabeth. "It was a good church."

A sturdy breeze stirs and with it a sheet of acorns rains down from above. We all scamper into the house, laughing, shrieking, avoiding the bombardment. Elisabeth prods me further for more details, but I am reticent—mostly because I'm lazy, but partly because I don't know how to verbalize the experience I've just had and because, I admit, I like to have a few secrets. She's used to it. I think secrets are healthy for a marriage—unless you're trying to cover up an affair or the fact that you're a licensed-to-kill double agent for a communist superpower.

I play with Jeremy for a little while. Elisabeth does some sewing. We eat lunch, then it's nap time for Jeremy. Mama takes him upstairs. I putz around, check emails, pick up a fly-fishing magazine, and fall asleep reading it. After everyone wakes up, we decide to go for a walk around the lake. Jeremy hops in the stroller. Lilly gets a leash. Mama and Papa gather water bottles, sunglasses, and walking shoes. We glide around the lake, offering humble salutations to the resident ducks, geese, and turtles. Under these circumstances, I drop down to a fairly normal mode of being—no fireworks, no earthquakes, but no problems or worries either. It's nice. We return, fix and eat dinner, and do our evening routine.

Old Dreams

It's four a.m. I can't sleep. Don't know the reason for this. Middle age? Melatonin deficiency? I've synchronized my circadian rhythm to the bass in my lake? I dunno. Well, since it's so early, and safe to say that Jeremy and Elisabeth are still sleeping, I want to show you something; follow me . . .

Here is the first of seven "how-to" steps on the path I traversed, which made it possible for me to arrive at *magic something*. I'm using quotes on the words *how-to* because I don't want to mislead you: These steps are just glimpses, pieces of a larger puzzle that encompass a lifetime of seeking, yearning, intuiting. No exact instruction manual could or will ever do this journey justice. I've chosen these seven key moments because I believe they're archetypal. In other words, if you're going to make this journey, you too will be passing here.

Archetypal Step 1: Something Is Not Right

It's spring 1988, twenty-two years ago. I'm a freshman in college—Syracuse University in upstate New York. It's Saturday.

I'm bound for Canada in my roommate's Jeep Wrangler. It's a late start, maybe four in the afternoon. I'm restless, disturbed, depressed. My roommate is out of town and has left me with his keys. The other guys on the hall are having their typical Saturday night drinking and pot-smoking extravaganza. I'm not up to it. Not up to them. Not up to burying this feeling in drugs or partying. I just wanna get away, not from the feeling, but from those who deny the feeling, situations that deny the feeling. Far away. I want to be alone and sink into the aloneness. As a matter of fact, maybe I can find some secluded field or country drive where an alien mother ship might pick me up and whisk me off to some other planet. That'd be nice. Abduction.

It's getting dark now. Two hours north. Sixty-five miles an hour. *Where am I going? Why am I doing this? Why? Why? It always ends up this way. I can camouflage myself for a short while, then true colors shine through. I'm no joiner, no member of the club; definitely not a brother in a fraternity. It's always there, lingering in the background. Unhappy. Depressed. Not clinically. Existentially. Yes, existentially depressed. Something is not right. Is there something wrong with me, or is this a condition common to everyone only they're denying it, burying it, ignoring it? Just unhappy. No real reason to be. College. Friends. Family. Support. Money. Free Time. Intelligence. Not ugly. Not crippled. Not addicted. Every advantage. Yet . . . unhappy.*

I'll turn off here. Good enough. I don't wanna drive to Canada. Who am I kidding? What's in Canada? Single lane road now. Pitch black out. *Where the hell am I going? Drive. Drive. Remember the turns. Got it. Easy enough. Gravel road? Come on. Aha. That'll do. Bouncy turnoff. Good Jeep. No flat tires. Keep going. Farther. Farther.* Field. Nervous. *If I get stuck I'm screwed; lots of walking. Come on . . .*

Relief. Made it. I get out. Lock the car. I take a deep, gut-filling breath. The air pressure billows past my heavy heart and into my lungs. It's cold out. Cold on my lungs. Frost on my breath. My eyeballs even sting a little. The tall, stale, winter-deadened grass crunches beneath my feet. A little slippery. There's a hill. Damn cold. Should have brought a heavier jacket. *Where am I going? To the top of the hill dumb-ass. No, where am I going? What am I doing? Why am I here? Why am I unhappy? Why?!* I reach the top.

Behold: Above my head, far above, there is a firmament like no other. Vast. Clear. True high definition. Every constellation is out to play. Even faint gestures of stars can be seen. Millions of them. There's a sci-fi bonus: Strewn through and about and undulating over this beautiful firmament is a wispy Aurora Borealis. I lie down, oblivious to the wet, cold grass. I sink into the view, the incredible view. The sky! The starry sky! It's screaming at us every single day: Mystery! Mystery here! Space is infinite. This is a realm, not a place! A realm; made of dreams, made of mind, made of fanciful nothingness. After a while, I am empty of thought, empty of struggling, empty of trying to understand. I know what is true . . . for me. *Something is not right.* I must fix it. Yes, I am determined to fix it. I am not going to live like this. I want my heart back. I want my freedom. I want Happiness with a capital H.

An eon passes in about twenty-five minutes. I get up. Stiff. Cold. Tired. Stumble back to the Jeep. Ignite the engine. Ahhh. Heat. I'm heavy of heart because I have to go back. But I'm finished here. I did find something I was looking for. Yes, still unhappy, still existentially depressed. But I have something new. Something that I did not have before: Resolve.

It's a little after six a.m. now. Jeremy troops in. I've been writing. I set my laptop down. We embark upon the morning routine.

At about eight, he sprouts two horns over some shower/bath incident; the details are lost on me. He's at an age when the struggle between independence and neediness is constantly churning; at times his fuse overloads, resulting in a breakdown like this morning—in this case, crying, screaming, shouting. I, too, get angry over the situation and erupt with a few terse words.

Some explaining: I may have access to this state of "peace that passeth all understanding," but it by no means exempts me from the entire range of emotion. Actually, I would say, if anything, I am freer to express these emotions more directly. I don't hold back. When I am mad at the dog, I am damn mad at the dog. When I am angry at someone, I can be raging angry. I froth. I curse. The anger comes, then it swiftly goes. No lingering. There's a perfect example of this type of behavior in the movie *The Lord of the Rings: The Fellowship of the Ring*. It's near the beginning of the movie. Gandalf (the wizard) has just arrived at Bag End and is visiting Bilbo Baggins in his hillside abode. In the scene, Gandalf is having difficulty convincing Bilbo to hand over the ring. Bilbo, of course, is reluctant to part with it. Gandalf erupts into a fierce, pure, field of rage. Cinematically, this is shown by some special effect in which Gandalf grows larger than he already is. He then subsides back to his normal size and returns to his wise and loving self. It's a beautiful and very powerful moment. We are given a peek into the true immensity of Gandalf's powers. Well, I don't have powers, but the emotional release that occurs within *magic something,* is very similar.

At nine thirty I leave for a customer's house. It's a private residence for which I've been contracted to install a surround-sound system. Today I'm doing the prewire. It's easy work. I'm in and out in about three hours. I'm on my game this morning. One of the ongoing benefits of *magic something* is performing its job beautifully today: I'm direct, quick, and efficient, straightforward, polite, and giving—everything a professional should be. It's easier to be this way with a little secret assistance. I say secret because, of course, I'm not blabbering on to the customer about my state. I'm just in the moment. The now moment—nothing better.

Next stop is lunch. I drive over to the shopping district near my house and enter Panera Bread; a slick corporate hive masquerading as a hip indie joint if there ever was one. I get in line. In front of me are several skinny dressed-in-all-black musician types. Authentic ones, I notice. Ostentatiously hanging from each of their black leather, metal-stud-encrusted belts is an all-access backstage pass with the name of some band I've never heard of emblazoned on it. I lean down to get a closer look. "Rat-a-Tat-Tat." Hmmm. Interesting name.

"You guys have a gig here in town?"

"Huh?"

Wake up guys. It's noon.

One of them realizes that the putz behind them is speaking to them. "Eh, yeah. We played at the Paramount last night."

"Was it a good show?"

"Yeah, we opened for Rat-a-Tat-Tat."

"Never heard of them. What kind of music is that?"

"Eh, sort of psychedelic, techno rock."

"Cool. Full house? Doesn't the Paramount hold about a thousand people?"

"Yeah, something like that. It was full."

"Well, glad you guys had a good time. This is a cool town. Lots of music here."

"Yeah. Thanks."

"I'll look you up online."

"Sure, man. Take it easy."

I order my food, get it on a tray, and sit down. I'm engrossed in thought about my conversation. I didn't get the name of their band, so I'm thinking about heading over to their table and making a fool of myself. I resist. Because, basically, I don't care . . . anymore. Anymore, because essentially I just came face to face with my old dreams, with my past.

I'm a musician. My fifteen-minute claim to fame was when I wrote a rock musical and had it produced in the Washington, DC, area around the turn of the millennium. It received good reviews. I wrote the story. I wrote the music. I produced the show. After the production came and went, I recorded a CD, had a video made, and got myself a slick PR agent in Hollywood to promote it to the entertainment industry. And there it fizzled. It took a long time to fizzle—about ten years to be exact. Trips to New York City. A revised production. More music. More videos. More. More. More. Until finally, I let it and my desired music career completely fizzle—into the grave.

So here I am in Panera Bread, face to face with my past. I'm completely ambivalent and here's why: No amount of *that* was ever going to give me what *magic something* gives me right here, right now. No doubt, it's a pretty cool experience, being on a stage with a guitar in your hand, volume at 11, and an audience seating to capacity. But when it's over, it's over. Conversely, the happiness derived from *magic something* is not dependent upon a damn thing. It's unconditional. Let 'em have the stage, the lights, the fans, and the fog machines. I'll take my version of heaven any day over that. Yeah, it took me about ten years to figure this one out. Never said I was smart, just persistent.

I finish my lunch, head out the door, and make the short drive back to the house. I say hello to the family, then walk down to my office. It's Monday, so I have some karma to pay. I begin some paperwork, Internet research, etc., then I get the phone call—from the Realtor with the 4.5 million-dollar property. Payback is hell. I summon my best bullshitting powers and try to convince him to let me do something with the property. He's nice enough and listens to my ideas for a short period. Eventually, however, he begins to smell the cattle excrement I'm dishing out and rudely hangs up on me. Oh, well. Tried. Out of my system now.

I don't really have much paperwork to do today, so I meander down to the pier and make a few casts. The day drips by. At five I have a phone webinar consultation with a company that promises Google search engine optimization. This is vital for my business. I do pretty well with Google through my own efforts, but there's no such thing as too much improvement in this area. It takes an hour. I learn a bit and decide to purchase further assistance from the company.

It's dinnertime now and time to wind down. The nightly routine rolls into action. I put Jeremy to sleep, say goodnight to Elisabeth, and hit the off button on the day.

The Clown

Not a lot happened today that you haven't already heard about. So instead, here's a short *magic something* story I think you'll like:

Once upon a time, there was a planet whose only inhabitants were clowns. Tall clowns with red noses and fuzzy hair. Short clowns with baggy pants and goofy hats. Medium-sized clowns with rainbow clothing and oversized red hands. Male clowns that danced on poles while somersaulting through the air. Female clowns that walked the high wire and swung from the trapeze. Hundreds of clowns. Thousands of clowns. Millions of clowns . . . all lived on this planet.

The only problem with these clowns is that they were very serious. Imagine that. A whole planet full of serious clowns. They did not smile, did not laugh, did not jump for joy. There was not a funny bone among them. But worst of all, these clowns did not love. Well, they knew a small kind of love, but it was usually limited to their families or closest friends. They did not love in the greater sense, which, of course, is the difference between a funny clown and a serious clown. One might say that these clowns were not very enlightened.

But at least they were smart clowns, because they knew they were not enlightened. They also knew that there were other planets out there that had enlightened clowns. Clowns that laughed and smiled and guffawed loudly. Clowns that loved, in the greater sense.

So one day, it was decided that one among them should go visit one of these other planets and bring back the secret that they all so desperately wanted. They gathered together one million of their finest colored balloons, strapped the lot to a spaceship, and sent their best astroclown on his way. Up, up, and away he flew. Past the clouds, through the atmosphere, beyond the moon, through the solar system, and finally out into the vast reaches of the galaxy. The clown floated for many years. Finally, he arrived at a tiny blue planet located in an obscure corner of one spiral arm of the galaxy.

The planet looked very promising. He gently steered his great multicolored balloon ship down toward one of the larger continents. He knew that not everybody on any given planet would be funny or loving in the greater sense, so with this in mind, he headed for the most probable places: hermitages, sanctuaries, monasteries—places, he had heard, that held the secrets he longed for.

He first visited a hermitage high in the snow-capped mountains; it housed hundreds of orange-robed monks with shaved heads. The clown had high hopes. He was not, however, greeted very cordially at the front gate.

"What do you want?" barked the monk. "We are a serious group here and do not have time for clowns."

The clown noticed that these beings communicated with their mouths, which was something very different from the way clowns communicated. Clowns spoke . . . well, by clowning: jumping, somersaulting, bouncing, flipping, gesticulating wildly with their arms and feet, etc. So when the clown tried to communicate to the monk, the monk stood there for a few seconds, then rudely slammed the door. The clown understood. This was not a place where he would find laughter or love, in the greater sense. So he turned around and continued his search.

The second place he visited was a monastery nestled in a verdant pastoral hillside. Once again, the clown's anticipation grew as he approached the front door. He knocked. Slowly the chains and locks were released, and the huge wooden door creaked open. There stood a brown-robed monk.

"What do you want?" barked the monk. "We are a serious group here and do not have time for clowns."

The clown spoke, and once again the door was slammed in his face. He moped back to his balloon ship. This was not going to be easy. *It may take years,* he thought to himself. But he had come this far . . .

The next place he visited was a small redbrick monastery adjacent to a small town. The gate was open. He walked up to the main doors and knocked. An elderly woman opened the doors and greeted him.

"Well, come on in, the door is open. Were you on the schedule today? I don't remember requesting a clown."

Though the clown didn't understand, he was happy to be at least through the doors.

"I tell you what, have a seat here, and we'll see what we can do."

He sat down and waited. A few moments later, the elderly woman returned and led him down a vast hallway to a large open room. They entered the room and all eyes went to the clown. In an instant, every monk in the room cheered and ran toward the clown with excitement. He was overwhelmed. He didn't know what to do, but when they all had gathered very close around him and settled down, he summoned his courage and began to deliver his message.

He had gotten no more than ten seconds into his speech when the most astonishing thing that had ever happened to the clown, or to any clown on his planet, occurred. Every single monk in the room cheered and laughed and guffawed and rolled over with tears of joy as he spoke. He had never experienced anything like it his whole life.

Laughing. Laughing! He thought to himself, *They are laughing!!* Then he, too, for the very first time in his life, laughed! Instantly, he realized the true nature of his own clown being: love, laughter, and freedom. He continued his speech, and, for hours, he and the monks delighted in one another's company. The day came to an end, and the clown was invited back the next day . . . and the next . . . and the next . . . and the next. . . .

The clown stayed until the end of a season when, finally, all the monks had to return to their individual villages for a short time. The clown knew that it was also time for him to return to his home. They said their heartfelt goodbyes, and the monks presented him with a certificate (of graduation, he presumed). He then floated away in his astroclown balloon spaceship, and it took many years for the clown to return to his planet.

When he arrived, he was very eager to share the good news. But first, he decided, it would be wise to translate the certificate the monks had given him. It was a big undertaking, but he and a small group of other science clowns finally translated the certificate. As he read it the clown laughed and laughed. In an instant, all of his clown peers began laughing. Soon, the entire clown planet had learned the secret of laughter and love, in the greater sense.

The certificate read:

Dear Mr. Clown,

Thank you! Thank you! Thank you for your daily doses of laughter and joy and extremely entertaining clowning! We will highly recommend your excellent services to others. Please come again! Bye for now, and Good luck!

Love,

The Third-Grade Graduating Class,
Thomas Johnson Elementary School

Options

You can struggle.

You can expend great amounts of effort and succeed.

You can expend great amounts of effort and fail.

You can hope, dream, and fantasize.

You can invest many years and finally make it.

You can invest many years and never make it.

You can slowly get there.

You can be an overnight success.

You can cheat and lie.

You can charm and cajole.

You can create and destroy.

You can build and tear down.

You can do, do, do, do, do, do, do, do.

You can do nothing.

You can practice, learn, gain, expand, improve, and grow.

But . . .

What most people never do—is almost the last thing anyone does—is accept.

No matter what the conditions.

Really, truly, deeply accept.

You'd be surprised what happens when you do this.

These are your options.

It's five a.m. When I was eighteen, five a.m. was a galaxy far, far away; at forty-one, it's a patch of dingy grass in my back-yard—way too ordinary. No one else is up, so I do some writing. You may have noticed that this is my preferred activity when awake at this time of day. I don't sit in silent contemplation. I don't do things like yoga, tai chi, or prayer. I don't try to enhance or perfect myself in any way. In other words, I've never been one who was inclined to get up early to partake in some method or technique that I thought would get me closer to *magic something*. It doesn't work that way. There is no logical sequence of steps you can take that will get you to the top of the mountain. Quite the opposite: It's about removing the steps and the mountain (sometimes painfully) and discovering that you *are* at the top. If this sounds vague, obscure, and obtuse, it is. Welcome to my strange wonderland. Eventually, yes, the view *is* quite nice.

It's one of those rare days that Jeremy and Mama sleep in. I migrate down to my office and stay there until about eight. I hear everybody getting up, so I amble upstairs to join them for breakfast. I eat quickly and begin to pack my stuff to head out to work. I have a home theater installation today. I'm getting a small knot in my stomach because I'm not feeling up for this routine performance today. Jeremy notices my packing and comments.

"Papa you going to work? . . . You a worker?"

Ugh. The boy calls it like it is. I'm bummed by this all-too-accurate description. It's a sore spot, because I wish I could be doing something else with my days. I groan and reply.

"Yeah, Papa is a worker bee, worker."

Elisabeth overhears, chuckles, and comments.

"Tell Papa he's a spiritual rock star."

Jeremy pauses, then does his best. "You a spirit rockin' stir, Papa?"

I smile from ear to ear. This cheers me up as I head out the door. Yep, I drill holes for a living; holes in ceilings, holes in walls, holes in floors—with fancy technology attached. That's about what it boils down to.

I began this job yesterday, so am already knee deep in it when I arrive. The details are prosaic, so I won't bore you. At about three p.m., I arrive at the oh-shit moment of the day, which has to do with a damaged underground cable. The circumstances dictate that I have some interaction with the general contractor, who is on site today and is probably the guy who damaged it. He's not my type. A little too militant, walled in, and stiff for my tastes. His local southern drawl doesn't add to his appeal either. We try a few things, go back and forth over options, and eventually he comes up with a Mickey Mouse solution that I don't like but agree to. Problem solved. Afterward, we linger around our trucks and talk as I'm packing up my tools. And that's when the "Second Coming" bomb hits.

This is one of the strange problems with *magic something*. I can't help but to give my complete attention and constant eye contact to just about anybody; even if that anybody is somebody I don't particularly care for. I've mentioned this before. It's because I have no agenda in these circumstances. No better place to be. No future moment I'm trying to get to which promises something better. I'm already feeling better. There is only now. Which is why it always strikes me as ridiculous when someone mentions the Second Coming.

We were having the usual "how hard it is to have your own business" conversation. There's an economic recession going on, so I do share a legitimate tough-times camaraderie with other small business owners. But when you give someone your complete attention long enough, sooner or later the conversation turns personal. Next thing I know, this guy is telling me about his wife, his sex life, his religious values, his kids, politics, you name it. I steer the conversation back to small business and make an uneducated guess that the recession will last until around 2013. I guess this was just too futuristic a number for this guy, because his response was this:

"I'm waitin' for the Second Coming. Maybe by then, won't have to worry 'bout none of that!"

"Eh, well, yeah . . . maybe . . . I don't know."

How am I supposed to respond ? I have no problem with the Second Coming as related to Jesus and the general gist that a more meaningful and fulfilling existence is possible. But when someone mentions *waiting* for the Second Coming, or Enlightenment if you meditate for twenty years, or world peace in the year 3000, or the great promises of the next political party, I have no response. The idea that personal happiness/fulfillment/salvation is waiting for us somewhere in the future is a wickedly illusory carrot. Chase it forever, but you will never get it, because *it* doesn't exist. It's a ghost. There is no such thing as the future.

When you're on a quest for *magic something*, one of the things you have to demand, to be successful in the least, is that whatever happiness/fulfillment/salvation there is, it must *be available* to you right now/this year/this decade/this lifetime. No more future. This is one of the greatest casualties, and greatest relief, should you decide to embark upon this quest. All of your schemes; all of your plans; all of your grandiose wishing, dreaming, and hoping; all of your controlling delusions telling you how you can make life bigger, better, and shinier—all of it—gets casually thrown on a pile of dry autumn leaves and burned to smithereens. Poof. Accepting who you are *now* is the only real course of action to take. Realize this fully, and you'll be amazed by the results.

I bid adieu to my general-contractor friend, hop in my car, and drive home. Elisabeth and Jeremy are sitting at the dinner table when I arrive. It's about six p.m. I join them for dinner, then head right back out the door. Today's theme must be delusion, because waiting for me this evening is interaction round two with a strangely future-idea-possessed individual—albeit a more sophisticated one. I signed up for this, so it's my own fault.

The search for the *magic something* switch takes you to all sorts of strange places. I accepted this a long time ago. I have no problem attending a Baptist worship, a Buddhist zazen, a Hindu satsang, or a Native American sweat lodge. If doing these types of things had been outside my social or religious comfort zone, I would never have made it to *magic something;* I'd bet against anybody who couldn't do this. If something has heart, I'm interested. I hold a simple premise: God and love are available to everybody. So tonight, I'm attending a gathering at a local coffee house that is for folks interested in a particular Americanized and modernized denomination of Hinduism called Advaita Vedanta. Google it. It's en vogue. There are a lot of teachers running around America currently offering their version of it. Like all religions,

Advaita Vedanta has an "experiential, heart and *magic something*" oriented side and a "conceptual, spin me round till I'm dizzy with stupid ideas" oriented side. I don't care what religion you practice, just choose the former side. This is why I'm baffled to no end about my own stupidity for attending this shriveled up/overintellectual/spin me round till I'm dizzy with stupid ideas gathering. At least the cup of joe was good.

I pull up to the coffee house. I'm spinning wildly out of control with *magic something,* so I make sure my head is attached and my pants are on before entering. Check. I'm excited. Maybe this is a group with whom I can actually share, talk a little about, openly confess these strange *magic something* days. I walk to the back of the coffee house and see the table where the group is seated. There are eight people: four women, four men. I say hello and take a seat. The group leader quickly introduces me to everyone, then we all take a moment to explain how and why we came to the meeting. It's a friendly gesture and nice to hear from similar souls. It takes about fifteen, twenty minutes to go around the table. I'm last to speak, and by the time my turn comes around, I'm not feeling too similar. Most of these individuals are half a century or older, and a good percentage of them are new to the topic at hand. I hesitantly and cryptically confess that I have been involved in these matters for close to twenty years, and the investment has paid off nicely. I leave it at that. I feel like a guy who shows up to the local Cessna flying club in an F-14 Tomcat.

Still, I am happy to be here; happy to engage in some deeper-than-usual conversation; and happy to meet new people. I'm ocean deep in *magic something.* Then the shenanigans begin. Ugh. The group leader has got it all wrong—conceptual, spin me round till I'm dizzy with stupid ideas wrong. Usually Advaita Vedanta gatherings like these are about heartfelt sharing and emotional resonance with some aspect of *magic something*. Instead, the leader announces the day's lesson plan, opens a ridiculously over-dog-eared and highlighted book, and launches into a discourse that might as well be about methane gas clouds on Jupiter. But it's not about methane gas clouds on Jupiter, which would be more interesting; it's about teacups.

Whether or not the teacups exist; whether our existence is the same as the teacups; whether we exist separate from the teacups; whether we exist outside the teacup; whether we exist inside the teacup; whether the teacup exists inside us; whether the teacups can grow fangs and bite the head off this guy; whether the teacups are existentially smarter than all of us—which, in my case, is a resounding yes, because I am on the verge of taking the teacup and smashing it on the leader's book and getting myself thrown out of this fine establishment.

Actually, I'm having only one thought: WTF does this have to do with anything? I do believe everyone else is also having the same or similar thoughts, but they don't know any better, and innocently enough, pretend to be enjoying this blood from a turnip operation. I'm not enjoying it. I can think of dental surgeries that were more fun. Eventually, during a lull in the diatribe, I meekly attempt to question the leader about his motives. It dents his enthusiasm only slightly, and he's soon back to his teacup hijinks.

The lesson to be gained from this silliness is this: Most people think that the search for *magic something* is about ever-increasing levels of complexity and sophistication, eventually arriving at some exclusive, glorious, and complex view of life, the world, and existence. In fact, it's quite the opposite: I don't view life from a multidimensional, 3D perspective. I'm utterly one dimensional. I reside on the shallowest and simplest of all possible levels. No grand visions. No deep philosophical insights. There are just me and my relationship to *magic something*. Is the switch on or is it off? When it's off, by god, I know it. It's painful; I'm suffering; I'm unhappy. When it's on, I'm at ease, I'm content, I'm happy. Reducing complexity to simplicity is the real challenge in the search for *magic something*.

Eventually, the leader's steam runs out, and the group takes over the discussion. Thank god. It's been torture. Not surprisingly, the conversation turns to the dubious nature of all this philosophizing. A few individuals have actually had the good fortune to be with authentic Advaita Vedanta *magic something*-realized teachers and are hip to the difference. Talk even ensues about getting one of these teachers to visit our little group.

The meeting comes to its conclusion. I linger a little and chat with a nice lady about a local church that we both occasionally visit. I depart, get in my car, and drive home. When I arrive, it's a little after nine. Jeremy is asleep already. I say hi to Elisabeth, then give her a kiss goodnight. It's been a long day. I'm liable to turn into a philosophizing, Second-Coming pumpkin soon. I crawl upstairs and put myself to bed.

Lollygagging

Let's talk about the second archetypal step on the journey toward *magic something*.

Archetypal Step 2: Proof and Faith

It's summer 1991, nineteen years ago. I just graduated from college and am free of the whole institutional educational thing. The real education now begins.

I'm underwater. I just jumped off a floating platform situated dead center in a lovely little country pond. The water is cooler down at this depth. I slowly surface and am embraced by the silky, warm top waters. I love ponds, lakes, rivers. I'll swim in these any day over a chlorinated pool. I pull myself onto the platform, find a spot, and lie on my back. The sun is high. The air is hot. Lollygagging would appropriately describe this experience. There are several other people here. We're all enjoying a respite from our very busy schedules of sleeping all day long. Well, not sleeping, but definitely lying in a bed, lights out, and eyes closed. I'll explain in a minute.

We all hear the sound of an old farm bell ringing in the distance. This means lunch. We take turns jumping back into the water and swimming to shore. I'm last to do so. I arrive at the small beach, towel down, and begin the long trek back to the center. I'm on a worn dirt path winding through cow fields, rolling hills, large oaks, and prickly, pink-flowered thistles. I take my time. There's plenty of food. It's being served cafeteria style, so no hurry. Eventually, I meet up with a gravel road and hop onto it. I can now see the roof of the center's main building looming over the next hill. I hear a car approaching. It's a pick-up truck. I continue walking on the gravel road. The truck pulls up alongside me. An elderly gentleman named Bob Monroe is driving. He rolls down the passenger-side window and looks at me with a twinkle in his eye.

"Need a ride back home?"

The question is obviously a joke. Where I'm headed is just a couple hundred feet away. He's not referring to that home. He's referring to another, grander, more philosophical abode: Home, with a capital H. I get the joke.

"No thanks. I can find own way back."

Indeed.

He smiles, rolls up the window, and continues on his way. Bob is a very cool guy. I was already impressed, but this seals the deal. I arrive at the main building where the cafeteria is, walk inside, and help myself to lunch. I only have about fifteen minutes before things get started.

I finish eating, then prepare for the afternoon session. I put on a comfortable t-shirt and some shorts, then head into the main gathering room. The group's leader tells us about the afternoon's objective. It's easy enough. We have a short discussion, then all head to our rooms. I turn out the lights and get in bed. I lie down, supine, and pull the covers up to my chest. I take the pair of headphones hanging on the adjacent wall and place them over my ears. Soon after, the main event begins. It's called Proof and Faith.

Faith that everything I'm doing here is benign, safe, and ultimately beneficial. Faith that if I actually succeed with this matter, it will give my *fix the something is not right* resolve a tremendous boost and advantage. Faith that if this is real, then the rest of *it* might be real. *It* being religion and spirituality and *magic something.* And Proof—that there actually, really is, beyond a shadow of a doubt, life after death.

Somebody somewhere in a back room has hit play, because I can now hear the sound of ocean waves in my ears. Then a gentle and matter-of-fact voice begins speaking. It's Bob Monroe again, this time prerecorded.

"You are more than your physical body."

Following this introduction, the binaural beats begin. You can barely hear them. A six hertz tone in one ear and a four hertz tone in the other. The brain synthesizes both of these tones into a third, entirely different one, which has the effect of quickly and efficiently putting me into a relaxed meditative state called alpha wave. The process is called hemi-sync, short for hemispheric synchronization. Google it. There are a million variations on the market. I'm not going to pretend that I understand all the scientific details of this process. All I know is that it works. Within a few minutes, I am deeply relaxed. Bob's voice comes and goes throughout the hour-long session, guiding me to the goal and point of all of this: an out-of-body experience.

Yes, you read that correctly: an out-of-body experience. I was never the type who could merely read a few words from the Bible or Bhagavad Gita or Koran (choose your sacred text) and easily believe it. Faith never came easily, probably because I was just more scientifically than religiously minded. I needed proof. It just seemed a matter of basic logic, that for me to believe in any of the larger concepts that the world's religions touted, I needed definitive confirmation of *one* very basic element they all had in common: belief in life after death. There were cures for skeptics like me, and Bob Monroe would be the doctor providing it.

When I first read Robert "Bob" Monroe's very well-known and critically acclaimed book *Journeys Out of the Body*, I knew that I had found a way to confirm this one very basic tenet. If I could have an out-of-body experience (hopefully multiple times), it would provide enough evidence for me to believe in life after death. If I could confirm this, then I would give religion and spirituality a closer, more thorough inspection. Proof first, faith second. *Proof and Faith.*

If all this sounds cultic or New Agey or outside your religious or social comfort zone, then just weigh it against your desire to find the *magic something* switch. Personally, I had no option; the desire for *magic something* was too strong, and, consequently, it made these sometimes strange and uncomfortable risks easier. Ultimately, indeed, there is nothing to fear but fear itself.

I don't have an out-of-body adventure today. The session comes to an end, and we break for a mid-afternoon discussion. It's all good. I'm here to learn and, with any luck, yes, fly to the moon. The day continues. We have another session in the late afternoon, followed by dinner, then an evening discussion.

I purchase a set of hemi-sync tapes to take home with me. Within six months, I do begin having out-of-body experiences; measurable, repeatable, definitely not a dream or wishful thinking, and nothing fancy—on most occasions, I merely float around the room. It's enough proof for me.

The Fisherman

There was once a fisherman who fished in the same pond week after week, month after month, year after year. He did not fish any other waters. He did not attempt to catch any other fish. He had been fishing in this little pond for nearly twenty years. The idea of fishing in any other place annoyed and agitated him tremendously. He only believed in this little pond.

Every now and then, his only friend, Edward, would invite him to go fishing on the nearby lake . . . or the ocean, even. (The fisherman had only one friend because, outside work and home, the little pond was the only place he ever went.) This invitation always elicited a sour response from the fisherman.

"Fish are fish. Why hassle around getting to the lake? Same fish, same worms, same hook . . . no thanks."

The truth of the matter was that the fisherman was tremendously frightened to go to any other pond or to any other body of water at all. The newness of it; the strangeness of it; the ridicule he might receive from others—all of this frightened him. He might drown. He might get lost. He might never find his way home again. It was much safer to just stay put and fish his little pond.Edward, of course, eventually stopped asking. Only once did the fisherman wonder why Edward never came around anymore. But, ultimately, the fisherman didn't care.

Fine, he said to himself, *just means I get the whole pond and the fish in it to myself.* His isolation from the world, on the little pond, was complete.

As one might imagine, the fisherman would often catch the same fish over and over again. One particular fine Saturday afternoon, the fisherman was on his pond, and, as luck would have it, he caught the biggest fish in the pond. (The fisherman thought he had caught this fish many times before, but it was years ago when the fish was smaller.) The fisherman heaved and struggled to bring in the big goliath. Finally, he hauled the fish onto his little boat. The fisherman could not believe his eyes, not because the fish was so huge or because he recognized the fish, but because the fish actually seemed to be trying to speak. So it was extremely disconcerting to the fisherman when, upon taking the hook out of the fish's mouth, the fish said this:

"Frank"—the fisherman's name was Frank—"you've been fishing in this pond for about twenty years now, and this is the fourteenth time you've caught me. I know that doesn't speak much about me, but I'm a fish. You're not. Don't you think it's kind of pathetic that this is the only pond you go fishing in?"

The fisherman was frightened out of his mind and couldn't comprehend what was happening. He immediately threw the big fish back in the water and, in a state of extreme agitation, rowed back to shore and went home.

A few days later, he thought to himself, *Surely I was dreaming, or delusional . . . or maybe, too much sun . . . or maybe too much to drink the night before. Yes, too much to drink.*

The following week, with just a tiny bit of apprehension, he headed down to the pond, rowed out into the middle, and began casting. Within minutes, he had a fish on the line. It was a big one. He reeled and fought and heaved. With one last burst of effort, he hauled it aboard. What he saw caused a ripple of fear in the fisherman unlike any he had ever felt. He paled. It was the same big, talking fish. The fish wriggled the hook out of its mouth and said:

"Frank, you've been fishing in this pond for about twenty years now, and this is the fifteenth time you've caught me. I know this doesn't reflect well upon me, but I'm a fish. You're not. Don't you think it's kind of pathetic that this is the only pond you go fishing in?" And with that, the fish jumped into the water.

The fisherman rowed to shore and went home, agitated, frightened, and very disturbed.

A couple of years went by. The fisherman did not fish. Finally, one day he was so bored and depressed that he summoned the courage to go fishing on the pond. He didn't even take out his boat. He walked up to the bank and timidly cast out. Immediately the fisherman began hauling in a fish. Yes, the big fish. This time, before the fisherman could even finish reeling him in, the fish took the hook out of its mouth, swam up to the shoreline, and said:

"Frank, you've been fishing in this pond for about twenty-two years now, and this is the sixteenth time you've caught me. I know this doesn't—"

"Who are you?! Is this some sort of joke?!" The fisherman interrupted, overcoming his fear.

"—reflect well upon me, but I'm a fish."

"I said, what is going on here?" The fisherman insisted.

The fish paused, then looked up at the fisherman and calmly continued: "You're not. Don't you think it's kind of pathetic that this is the only pond you go fishing in?"

"Well, I happen to enjoy fishing in this pond!" the fisherman replied. "This is my pond, and I fish here whenever I want! A . . . aaaand I f . . . f . . . fish in other ponds too!" The fisherman couldn't believe what he had just said. "That's right! I'm goin' fishing in the lake tomorrow! Stupid #$!!@ fish!"

Just then, the big fish swam back out into the pond.

"Stupid fish!"

A few years later, the fisherman was returning from a fishing trip at the lake with Edward, and because he had some spare time, he decided to go down to his old pond, which he hadn't been to in years. He got in his boat, rowed out a few feet, and began casting. As soon as the lure hit the water a huge fish took hold. The fisherman fought and struggled and finally hauled the fish aboard. This time, the fisherman was not surprised or afraid.

"Frank, you've been fishing in this pond for about twenty-four years now, and this is the seventeenth time you've caught me. I know this doesn't reflect well upon me, but I'm a fish. You're n-o-o-o-o—"

The fisherman calmly flipped the fish over on its back and pushed the spot that Edward had told him to push. A compartment opened up, two batteries rolled out, and the fish went silent.

The fisherman looked up and, noticing for the first time in many years just how beautiful his little pond was, thought to himself, *Fish don't talk.*

And with that he rowed his little boat to the shore, packed up all his gear in his truck, and rambled down the driveway . . . making his way toward the big beautiful ocean . . . where he and Edward were going on a two-week fishing trip—with other fisherman he had never meet, on waters he had never fished, and with strange new fish he had never caught.

The fisherman was secretly hoping that maybe, just maybe, he'd catch a fish that really did talk.

Lions and Tigers and Bears, Oh My

It's five thirty a.m. Saturday, and today, I . . . um . . . am goin'
fishin'—not allegorically but really, with a rod, reel, lure, and
boat. I'm going with a friend of mine who has a Jon boat and a
knack for catching really big bass. I can't wait.

My friend calls at about five forty-five. He can't go because of
some work-related issues. So I think it through—I'm still going,
come hell or high water. I've got a golden pass from the wife to
do this, and I ain't skipping the opportunity. My fishing gear is
all packed and ready to go. I have a recreational kayak in a kayak
rack on the roof of my car. I'm set. It's about six now. I pull out
of the driveway. I should be on the water by six thirty. As I leave,
I can see the faint cadmium glow of the dawning sun on the
eastern horizon.

I arrive at my friend's top-secret, deluxe spot on the local
river and get my gear ready to go. It's an easy haul down to the
water. *Magic something* in this instance is a superfluous notion
or experience, because fishing (experienced properly, for me at
least) already invokes this state. Take it from this fellow, Henry
David Thoreau: "Many go fishing all their lives without knowing
that it is not fish they are after."

Well stated. But, admittedly, it *is* nice to catch a fish or two, or forty-two. As I launch my kayak into the water, I slip down the steep wet bank and enjoy an early morning mud bath. Ugh. It gets everywhere—pants, shoes, shirt sleeves, hands. Oh, well. Don't need to worry about keeping clean now.

I'm in and take my first paddle strokes. Fog tendrils are steaming off the river. No one else is around. The only sounds I hear are chattering birds, probably discussing the strange, floating, yellow thing in the river. It's nice. I reach around to the brain-off switch (did I tell you about that one?—just kidding) and gently guide myself deep into the mystery of nature, god, and now. This is my favorite thing to do in the whole wide world. Jeff disappears. All traces of effort disappear. All that remains is the slow movement of the universe: paddling, drifting, listening, breathing, looking, being, fishing.

I float to a spot that looks good. I pull out the fishing pole tucked at my feet. It's a Field and Stream, black, six-and-a-half-foot, fiberglass, medium-fast action rod with a Quantum bait-casting reel—for you fishing geeks. I love it. It's lightweight, responsive, and can easily handle a four- to five-pound bass. Not that I've caught a five-pound bass with it yet—maybe a three pounder—but I have faith that when I do, it'll perform just fine. I'm using an artificial lure called a spinnerbait, with a pearly white, double-tailed plastic worm attached to the hook. (I never use live bait—that's not sport, that's cheating. And I practice catch and release only. Yes, I'm a fishing snob and proud of it.) I make my first casts toward the bank, and my contentment meter skyrockets.

All this leads me to a little *magic something* teaching. Today, I have with me *two* rod-and-reel outfits. One is the aforementioned, Field and Stream/Quantum setup. The other is also a Field and Stream, but it's a old, seven-foot, heavy-action model with a Zebco closed-faced reel. An odd thing occurs with this rod and reel today: I use it, and it's awful. It's clunky, heavy, and nonresponsive. It casts as if it were a string on a log and is about as accurate as a shotgun. Yet two months ago when I was using this rod, it felt and worked *just fine*. Nothing about it has changed.

The obvious reason for this conundrum is that I just started using the more refined rod about a month ago, so my sensitivity and handling expectations have changed. This is the perfect metaphor for what one goes through before finding the *magic something* switch and turning it on: You must become sensitive to the fact that the fishing pole you are using is a total piece of crap. Of course, this is easier said than done, because doing so is often a painful process. It's no joy to discover that who you are and how you feel is the equivalent of a crappy fishin' pole. As a matter of fact, most people do everything in their power *not* to discover this. But sooner or later, if you're a smart fisherman and truly care about catching more and bigger fish, you'll change poles.

Okay, now because I have no self-control, I'm gonna tell you *the* fish story . . . er, uh . . . animal story . . . from this trip: The sun is up now, and I'm about mile upstream from the boat slip. I've caught a couple of fish by this point but nothing big. A place in the river characterized by a large S-shaped bend is coming up. I approach. A fox jumps and scurries away on the bank to my right. Then, a loud splash. As I enter the bend, I see three buck white-tailed deer scramble into the water and make their way across. The water is deep here, over their heads. I've never seen deer swimming before and am delighted by the show. They quickly and efficiently swim across the pool and climb out onto the far bank.

Then, just when I thought this animal kingdom display couldn't be any cooler, I spot a bald eagle in a large dead branch on a tree on the left bank. Damn, now that's cool. The eagle sees me and takes flight, soaring upstream to the next branch. I scramble to get out my camera, continue paddling, and prepare to take a picture as I approach his new perch. I see him clearly. Closer. Closer. I push the camera button a few times and capture a shot of him in the tree. Nice. Crunch. Crackle. Crunch again. What the hell is that noise? I've got the camera up to my face. Get closer to the eagle. Paddle stroke. Closer. Camera still in my hand. Closer. Crunch. Okay? What the hell is that noise coming from the left bank? I turn my head and neck about one hundred and ten degrees backward and—oh, shit! Black bear! On the bank. Sixty feet away. Oh, shit! Calm down. He's not interested. Keep eye contact. No jerky movements. Snap the photo! Snap the photo! He's just walking. Shit, he must be two hundred to two hundred fifty pounds. I hold the camera to my face again, but—damn it, the current has me now. Too far. Try the zoom! Just take the shot! Snap. Snap. Oh, well. We'll see. I look back to where the eagle was perched. Of course, gone now. The black bear recedes into the verdant distance. I float away.

And that's my story: black bear, bald eagle, three buck white-tail deer, and a red fox—all in about five minutes. I love fishin'. Fishing has gotten me to some pretty amazing places and some pretty amazing circumstances. Maybe an hour or two later, I catch my biggest smallmouth bass of the fishing season—on my new pole, of course.

Around midday, I return home and have the happy pleasure of telling Jeremy and Elisabeth about my fishing adventures. Jeremy, at three years old, is excited to bursting point about my animal adventures and questions me about it for the rest of the day. A lazy afternoon filled with toy diggers, rocks, a walk to the park, and a nap ensues. Around dinnertime, we fire up the barbecue, set up the dinner table on the outside deck, and enjoy a late fall evening. Soon afterward, everybody heads upstairs, and Jeremy is eventually coaxed into bed.

The last event of the day is in . . . uh . . . stark contrast to this morning's nature adventures: Elisabeth and I watch *Iron Man 2*. An enjoyable, clever movie with just enough self-awareness and self-deprecating humor to be considered intelligent. But read between the lines, and you'll perceive the movie's real message, which is definitely in cahoots with the temperament of the modern world: Happiness can be attained through gadgets, technology, and *stuff*. Even with it's self-mocking, quasi-intelligent quality, *Iron Man 2* stinks of a pedantic, myopic, materialistic ethos which is ruining this world. I'm ranting I know, but it was the summer box office's number one movie.

Beddy-bye time.

Festival

Sunday. I'm up six thirty. I'm also a little hung over. Too much rich food and beer last night. Elisabeth gets up around seven. She didn't sleep very well. She's a little cranky. That's two strikes. Jeremy seems to be okay, but shortly, following our excellent adult guidance, he too slips into the cranky strike zone. It's a cranky festival . . . Sunday with the Cranks! Yeah! This is perfect because today we actually *are* going to a festival—the Graves Mountain Fall Art Fair and Festival. Yahoo! We decided we'd do this last night. We usually try to reserve our family outings for the mornings because Jeremy still takes naps, which tend to bog down afternoon activities. Mornings are always easier for this type of thing. We eat breakfast and slowly work our way out of the collective crankiness. The festival is about an hour's drive away, so we scramble and fuss and pack and double check, then, finally, are out of the house by nine thirty.

It's a nice drive through the foothills of the Blue Ridge Mountains. We arrive and are guided by rangers to park in a big grassy field. I'm astonished at the number of people already on the grounds—hundreds. In the grand scale of things, this is just a little local festival—a dime a dozen—so the attendance is impressive. I hop out of the car. Jeremy, check. Wife, check. Jacket, check. Wallet, check. *Magic something,* check. Jeremy and I have been here before, about a year ago, for a fishing festival. I've also fished plenty of times in this neck of the woods, so I am familiar with the place. The grounds and buildings sit beside a cute little trout stream that meanders down from the Blue Ridge Mountains. It's the focal point of the place. Well, I'd like to think so, at least.

We head over to the main area where the community building, art booths, and activities are situated. It's a cornucopia of country sight, smell, and sound, and I take it all in through the blissful filter of *magic something.* Biker dudes with leather pants and pony tails. Country dudes with cowboy hats and blue jeans. Farmer dudes with overalls and muddy shoes. Redneck dudes with camouflage hunting shirts and baseball caps. City dudes with collared shirts (tucked in) and matching socks. Hippy dudes with tie-dye t-shirts and torn blue jeans. Bluegrass dudes with banjos and skinny necks. Civil War reenactment dudes with muskets and flannel pants. Everybody is here. I take them all in—not offended, bothered, or annoyed. Not preferring one type over another. Not jealous or envious. Not with love or without love. Not with joy or hatred or judgment. I just see them. I'm totally aware of them. I can look all of them in the eyes and know that they are, in truth, my brothers, my sisters, my family—the human race. How strange we all are in our particular getups. And I'm no different. I'm the *magic something* fisherman dude. It's a good day. It's Sunday. I'm in church again.

We browse and make a few small purchases. Jeremy and Mama become occupied at a booth that makes and sells colored sand–filled bottles for kids. I go off on my own to inspect the rest of the show. I grew up going to these type of festivals, so I'm pretty efficient when it comes to getting in and out of booths. Most of the arts and crafts here are amateurish, but a few booths shine. I join up with Elisabeth and Jeremy again. We find a lady from Ghana selling handmade baskets. They're beautiful, so we buy one.

It's time for lunch. I'll skip the details except for one, because it lends itself to some *magic something* teaching. We sit down to eat in a crowded, covered, open-air facility, where mothers and fathers and children are all seated trying to make order out of a chaos. We're eating. I glance at a nearby table, and there I see it. Sitting across from me is another human being who is clearly in the *magic something* state. She is at peace. She is calm, settled, and content. She is wide eyed, open, and happy. She is seated and relaxed. And . . . she has an ice-cream cone in her hands, which she is eagerly devouring . . . thus the reason for her *magic something* state.

Here's the teaching lesson: There's no mystery going on here. We all know pleasure. We all know satisfaction. We all know the happiness that comes from *things.* But here's the catch: I bet that woman is totally unconscious of her current altered state. She's aware of the sensation the ice-cream cone is producing. She's aware of its taste on her tongue. She's aware of the pleasurable swallow. But what's she's probably *not* aware of is the whole context in which it's taking place. In other words, probably like the rest of her life, she's lost in it. Identified with it. Slapped around by it. A slave to it. She's not the master of the moment. The ice-cream cone is the master. She is not observing herself eating the ice-cream cone. She doesn't distinguish herself from the act, the observer from the experience. She is *lost* in the experience. And that is the lesson. You can have thousands upon thousands of pleasurable moments (cigarette, anyone?), but unless you can separate yourself from them, you will always essentially be a slave to them and thus destined to repeat them over and over again. In other words, to arrive at a permanent state of *magic something,* you must be willing to extract yourself from the matrix of the world, because *magic something* is beyond the world. Last thought and then I'll stop: Finding *magic something* requires that you realize the fundamental essence of who you truly are: the empty vast awareness behind your thoughts, your emotions, your likes and dislikes, your desires, your world. Not as easy as it sounds, but well worth it. Okay, that's it.

It's been a fun morning. After lunch Elisabeth, Jeremy, and I walk around a bit more, then decide to take off. We stop on our way out to listen to some bluegrass music. It must be a sign of old or middle age, but damn if I don't like bluegrass. I'm a rocker at heart, so this has a been slow revolution. I stand there like a fool, then dance with Jeremy. I apparently run up against a socially unacceptable wall here in country-bumpkinville, because I'm getting some pretty funny stares. *Oh come on!* I think to myself, *It's bluegrass music.* Sadly, Jeremy and I are the only ones in a sea of people who are groovin' to the jingly-jangly tunes. We slowly walk away and melt into the remains of the day.

It's a quick jaunt back to the house. Jeremy falls asleep en route. We pull into the driveway, and Elisabeth successfully transfers him, asleep, to his bedroom. We transfer ourselves to our bedroom, and everybody takes a nap. The day runs its course with all the usuals—rocks, diggers, games, dogs, cats, dinner, bedtime, movie, teeth brushing, pulling back the covers, closing the eyes, receding back into the great void of sleepy nothing awareness.

The Crane

To my supreme delight, I have just learned that the word commonly used to describe the endowment of animals with human characteristics is called anthropomorphizing. Fascinating. I have never really understood why humans use this strange ploy, but they do. My name's Pendleton. I'm a crane, and I have a story for you. It's called *The Four Cranes*. Yes, I know—another strange one—a crane spinning a yarn to be read by humans, about cranes who are representing humans, all because humans find it easier to learn something if a member of the animal kingdom bears the burden first. Go figure. Here's the story.

The Four Cranes

Once upon a foggy time, there were four cranes who, during an early morning descent pattern into a secluded swampy inlet of western Missouri's Lake Winnebago, were swiftly killed by a loud barrage of buckshot, fired by three elderly sportsmen crouched in a duck blind. They had mistaken the cranes for a large gray flock of green-winged teals. One, two, three, four—each of the cranes fell like great chunks of charred granite, right out of the sky.

Upon death, the four cranes were surprised to find themselves seated in a strange waiting area where a long line of assorted waterfowl had formed in front of a large, pearl-encrusted gate. Shortly, each of them was handed a number and told to get in line. So they did. They waited and waited, until finally the first crane made it to the pearly gates. There, seated at an old oak desk, was a hoary, majestic-looking snow goose. He introduced himself.

"Hello. I'm St. Petrovich, keeper of the gates of waterfowl purgatory. From here, you will enter either heaven or hell. I have for you, just one question. Please, if you would tell me, what is the definition of heaven?"

The first crane looked rather taken aback. He thought about it for a moment, then replied: "Easy. Heaven is a large beautiful lake with a never-ending supply of fish and frogs that jump right into my mouth whenever I desire!"

"Hmmm," St. Petrovich replied. "Hell it is."

In an instant, before the first crane could say another word, he vanished into thin air.

"Next," said St. Petrovich.

The second crane, having overheard their conversation, walked hesitantly up to the gate.

St. Petrovich spoke: "Hi there. I'm St. Petrovich, keeper of the gates of waterfowl purgatory. From here you will enter either heaven or hell. I have for you, just one question. Please, if you would tell me, what is the definition of heaven?"

The second crane was a little nervous and took more time to think through his answer.

He finally replied: "Heaven is a large beautiful lake with a never-ending supply of fish and frogs and absolutely no hunters!"

"Hmmm," St. Petrovich replied. "Hell it is."

In an instant, the second crane also vanished.

The third crane was squirming with fear as he approached the pearly gates. He too had been listening in on the fate of his friends.

St. Petrovich spoke: "I'm St. Petrovich, keeper of the gates of waterfowl purgatory. From here you will enter either heaven or hell. I have for you, just one question. Please, if you would tell me, what is the definition of heaven?"

The third crane was sweating shotgun pellets. This was rather easy for him, as he still had a few lodged in his forehead. He thought, and he thought, then answered: "Heaven is a large beautiful lake with a never-ending supply of fish and frogs . . . that I will, eh, share with all my friends and relatives! . . . and there won't be any hunters! . . . and—this was the part he was most proud of and was sure would gain him entrance into heaven—there's peace and harmony and happiness and fun for everyone who lives there!"

St. Petrovich took a deep breath. Paused, sighed, then spoke: "Hell—"

"No!!!" shouted the third crane.

". . . it is," said St. Petrovich.

And the third crane vanished.

The fourth crane slowly walked up to the gate. He had overheard the fate of his friends.

"Spare me the introduction," he blurted out.

"Heaven is a lake where some days the fishin' is good, and some days the fishin' is bad. Some days I feel like eatin' all the fish myself, and some days I feel like sharing it with my friends. Some days I'm a happy crane and love my fellow crane brothers and sisters, and other days I'm a cranky crane and want to peck their eyeballs out. There are hunters."

St. Petrovich smiled. "That doesn't sound anything like heaven."

"Yeah I know, but when you send me to hell, at least I know what I'll be getting and who I'll be."

St Petrovich smiled again. "So you think heaven is knowing who you are, and accepting the truth of things?"

"Yeah. That sounds about right," said the fourth crane.

"Sounds about right to me, too," said St. Petrovich. "Back to the lake ya go . . ."

And with that, the fourth crane vanished.

Then St. Petrovich did a very strange thing. He looked out upon the horizon and almost as if he were talking to some unknown mysterious person, he spoke:

"Hello there—yes, you with the book in your hands. Yes, *you*—reader. If heaven is knowing who you are . . . then . . . I have for you just one question: Who is the main character in this story? Not me. I'm not real. A talking snow goose named St. Petrovich? The author made me up. You don't think the four cranes are real do you? The author made them up too. Certainly there is no crane named Pendleton telling this story. So, I'll ask you again: *Who* is the main character in this story? Who is the one voicing and speaking all the parts? Who is speaking them now? Me? A crane? The author? Who is that awareness? Who is reading and thinking right now? That's right, you are. *You* are the main character. Your awareness is the *same* awareness in all the characters, including mine, the four cranes, the author's, and Pendleton's. There is only One main character . . . shared by all. There is only One awareness. Here's the lesson: It's the same in everybody. It's the same awareness . . . Heaven is knowing who you are."

And with that St. Petrovich vanished.

Pendleton here. Good little yarn, eh? Anthropomorphizing. Very interesting stuff. Well, it's been nice. I'm off; it's dinner time. Time to go fishin'—again.

Sinking Ship

It's six a.m., and I'm down by the lake. Time to go fishin'—again. I decided to go kayaking this morning, but today, dear reader, you're not coming along. While I'm fishing, you're going to investigate the third archetypal step on the journey toward *magic something.*

Archetypal Step 3: Fear and Courage

It's December 19, 1997, fourteen years ago. It's movie time.

I'm driving around the shopping district with my friend Miles at about ten p.m. We were just in a Borders bookshop, purchasing a few Christmas presents. Time to kill. I suggest we go see a movie. This was back in the day when, if you wanted to know what time a movie began, you either called the theater (with dubious results) or you just got in your car and drove. We drive. I pop out of the car and run into the theater while Miles waits. Eleven o'clock. That's when it starts. Cool. We go park the car, then scurry through the biting cold air into a loud, bustling, overcrowded cineplex. Bustling and overcrowded because, despite the fact that it's around ten thirty, there is a national—to be international—movie-going phenomenon taking place. It's called *Titanic*.

I don't need to describe this movie to you. No doubt you've seen it, perhaps multiple times. It's James Cameron's then Christmas gift to the world. We grab some popcorn and drinks and go sit down in the theater. No previews. You know a movie is big when the movie studio forgoes bombarding you with advertisements for their other movies. Fast forward to the part where the ship is sinking, and all aboard know that the inevitable is coming.

In a nutshell, *Titanic* is about death. I've been on the *magic something* path for about six years now, and if there's one thing I can tell you, it's this: Discovering your own *magic something* is also, in a nutshell, about death. I won't explain the details of this, but it's not hard to imagine that to discover *something* of this magnitude, other things are gonna have to give way. Other things are going to have to die. Thus, during the search for *magic something,* one encounters in a very real way, over and over again, the wall of one's own mortality, characterized by encounters with existential fear: fear of death, fear of annihilation, fear of isolation, fear of failure, fear of unhappiness, etc. Pretty heavy stuff. *Titanic* is also about some pretty heavy stuff. Tonight is a case where, against all odds, two objects with two different trajectories are going to collide. I'm not referring to the boat and the iceberg here. I'm referring to me and this movie.

The knot in my stomach started with the dancing scene in the engine room of the lower sections of the ship. Something about that scene triggered a very real knowledge of my own impending death. Existential death, not physical death. Existential death points to the death of ingrained notions, ideas, delusions—that you are a separate ghostly or disembodied entity trapped in a physical body and/or that you are a physical body trapped in the world. The true death of these ideas manifests with a tremendous amount of fear and consequently feels very much like physical death.

I am now sweating and growing pale and faint with fear. A cold chill settles over my body. I've got the shakes. Dread has filled my entire being. *What the hell have I done? Why did I go mucking around in these matters? What was I thinking? I've been diddling like a débutante in a whore house with the fabric of the universe, and it is now about to unravel, me along with it.* Tears of horror are forming in my eyeballs. I'm having trouble holding them back. I say something to Miles and stumble out of the theater. I walk on jelly legs to the exit and collapse to my knees out front. A few deep breaths of cold air. Miles follows. I'm crying now, garbling my words to Miles in an effort to explain. I'm not going back into the theater. Sorry. Got to me. Death. . . . He's understanding. We walk over to the car and get in. I'm a bundle of raw nerves. We head back to his place.

We arrive at Miles's apartment. I'm too fried to drive home, so I decide to spend the night. I lie down in the guest bedroom. I am still in the grip of a deep, dreadful existential fear. But for the first time, I take notice of something. I can literally feel awareness or consciousness moving across my brain, as if from the left hemisphere to the right hemisphere, as if for the first time spreading into new locations within my brain. I think to myself, *This* movement *is the cause of all the fear.* Knowing this doesn't alleviate the fear, but at least puts it into perspective. There's something biological about this mess I've gotten myself into, and it's completely out of my control. It's going to run its course whether I like it or not. Might as well relax. Stop trying to control. Stop trying to manipulate. Stop putting it off. This resolution helps a little, but by and large the fear remains, and I sleep fitfully throughout the night. It subsides by morning. I survive.

I thank Miles for letting me spend the night and get in my car. During the drive home, I realize . . . this will not be the end of it. This was the biggest encounter I've ever had with this beast, but it will be back. This I'm sure of. *At least,* I think to myself, *when it does come back, I will be able to handle it. I will have the courage to handle it. Yes I will.*

Miners

It's five thirty a.m. I'm up and writing. I don't spend too long doing this as there is something downstairs that is drawing my attention. I finish up and make my way down. I get the coffee started, then head into the dining room/office. I fire up the computer and log into CNN. I head into the living room, turn on the projector, and pull down the screen (I'm an audio/video installer, remember). The computer image shows up on the projection screen. Today is the conclusion of something that has had the deserved attention of the world for well over a month. Thirty-six trapped miners in Chili are being set free from their rocky underground tomb. Well, would-have-been tomb, had it not been for the quick action, ingenuity, and determination of a team of engineers hailing from countries all over the world. It's been pretty inspiring. Last night, before I went to bed, they were just about to begin the process of extraction. A capsule big enough to hold one miner was going to be slowly lowered into a hole two miles down to where the miners were located. None had been rescued before sleepy-time got me. Now at six a.m., five miners have been pulled up. The process is taking about two hours per minor, but it looks as though they will all be rescued.

Jeremy and Elisabeth eventually come down and the day begins. I don't have field work today, so I'm homebound. Around nine o'clock, I walk down to my office and get started. Nothing interesting here to report, so I think I'll comment further on the miners, since today is, after all, really *their* day.

There's an interesting corollary here. Of course, equating the miners' freedom to the freedom gained in discovering *magic something* is the obvious one. But that's not the corollary I'm referring to. It's this: Once you've attained freedom, then what? In other words, once you've had your fifteen minutes of harrowing fame, once you've been freed from the mine, once you've gone through the hero's journey . . . once you've discovered your own *magic something* . . . then what in the world do you do afterward?

I'm sure for the miners, the bliss of freedom and the temporary fame will be short lived. Then, it's back to the mines, so to speak. To a certain degree, this same thing happens after you've discovered *magic something*. However, no one is there to congratulate you, interview you, offer you a book deal, give you a diploma, or even high-five you. For the most part, *no one* is going to notice. *Magic something* and seventy-five cents won't even buy you a cup of coffee, because coffee costs well over a buck these days. The reward, of course, is self-validating, but it would be nice, in a fantasy world, to step up to a podium in front of thousands of people and receive a standing ovation for your efforts. It doesn't work like that, of course. Oh, well. Back to the day.

I continue to tackle today's office work until around lunchtime, then meander upstairs. I'm done and a little bored. Mama wants to do something on her own today, so I offer to watch Jeremy for the afternoon. We eat some lunch, then decide to head to the quaint walking district of the local downtown area . . . for some ice cream. I'm only semi-thrilled by this prospect, as I've been on this adventure with Jeremy a few other times, but it's a good way to pass the time, and the weather is pleasant. We get in the car and make the drive. We're soon strolling down the six or so blocks of the bricked-off downtown. We do the ice cream thing, the marble thing at the toy store, and the horsey thing on the carousel. It's nice, but probably like those miners who are now enjoying their newfound freedom and lives, I am saying to myself: *Now what?* I'm full-on into *magic something,* and can't share it with anyone. It's a feeling of being all dressed up and having nowhere to go. I'm getting desperate. I know a few people in this town. I look for somebody I know. Nobody. Not a soul. Damn, this sucks. I love being with Jeremy, of course, but the raw truth of *magic something* is that it compels you during and after the search for it to seek deeper meaning, deeper connection with others, and a deeper life purpose. Right now, despite the fact that I'm floating in a self-contained bubble of bliss, I'm longing for a deeper life purpose. Today is indeed a day to reflect upon freedom.

We wrap up our tour of downtown and drive back home. Jeremy falls asleep in the car. I pull into the driveway and open the doors to the car. I let him sleep. I get a lawn chair and set it up next to the car. The sun is just warm enough to warm my soul as I relax with a good fishing magazine. It's very pleasant. I too fall asleep. A little later, Elisabeth pulls into the driveway and soon afterward, everybody is awake from their naps. The day unfolds. By nine that night, all of the miners are free. I think I can feel their relief all the way up here on our continent, or maybe I feel the relief of the world because something good has finally happened, or maybe it's just *magic something* relief reflected back to me in the day's news. I don't know. Time for bed.

The Violin Master

If I were a serious student of the violin and had thousands of dollars at my disposal and could have any teacher in the world, I would seek out the most well-known violin master I could find and beg him to teach me.

If he said yes, and before I actually shelled out the big bucks, I would ask him: "Sir, are you or are you not a great violin master? For I pray that one day I too will be a great violin master. I would like to be assured that I am learning from the best. Is this not the case?"

Naturally I would hope for a quick response. I would only need to hear him say it once. Just once. Then, I would know.

"Yes, my child, I am the greatest violin master who has ever existed."

Excellent. Okay. And yeah, maybe I'd ask him to play a lick or two just to prove it. Hired.

But, if he had said: "Yes, child, I too learned from a great violin master and understand your longing. The path of a master is ongoing and one must be committed to the end. It's a pathless path, leading down a road with no beginning and ending, to an end with no ending."

Eh? . . . What? All I asked was: Are you or are you not a great violin master? Simple question. Pass. See ya. Bye.

And, if he had said: "No, child, I am not a violin master, but I have learned many useful things that I could teach you."

Well, okay, that's respectable, but I'm sorry, I am looking for and wish to be taught by a *great violin master.*

Sooner or later, in the search for *magic something,* you're going to need help. If this scares you or you aren't trusting (at least a little) or you downright refuse, you will fail. It's that simple. No teacher, no *magic something.* Okay, maybe one in two billion can do this without help. Not good odds. Personally, I wasn't willing to accept those odds, so I got help from everybody I could. Everybody, that is, who I thought was a real violin master. Here is the archetypal step in the search for *magic something* that covers this.

Archetypal Step 4: Instruction and Teachers

It's May, 1997, fourteen years ago, about eight months prior to the *Titanic*/Courage and Fear day.

Motel 6 is the same everywhere you go. The one I'm staying in now has the same drab, manufactured-not-to-offend, maroon carpeting and nondescript beige bed covers that are in all Motel 6s. But the blandness *is* offensive, sorta like an automated service satisfaction survey from your bank—service was good, until the annoying phone call. I'm up early because A) I still have jetlag from flying to northern California for the weekend, and B) I have a private appointment in about fifteen minutes with Steven and Felicia. (These are not their real names, and the same goes for the other names mentioned today.)

For simplicity and clarity, Steven and Felicia are *magic something* teachers. They would, however, probably deny such colorful nomenclature. Most teachers of this type are sensitive about vocabulary, terminology, and descriptive wording, simply because so much of what they do involves describing states that are impossible to describe.

Before leaving the motel, I grab my complimentary bland cup of coffee, muffin, and banana. I get into my tiny California rental car and zoom through the back streets of San Raphael. I arrive at their condominium complex in a few short minutes, get out of the car, and ring their doorbell. It's about eight o'clock. Felicia answers the door and welcomes me in. Steven meanders into the room. We have some friendly conversation, then begin. We walk into their simple, unadorned living room. There's a TV, a sofa, several cushioned chairs, a coffee table, some books, a few pictures on the walls. I sit on the couch. They sit in chairs opposite me. We close our eyes and sit in silence for about ten minutes. I'm feeling a little sleepy, but beyond this, I feel nothing extraordinary or strange. Steven rings a small bell and everyone opens their eyes. Then . . . we talk. That's the *magic something* teaching, believe it or not.

Okay, yes, it's slightly more than just talk: It's the deepest, most earnest type of talk two human beings can engage in, with questions like these: Why are you here? What are you looking for? What are you truly looking for? Who are you? Happy? Unhappy? Angry? Fearful? Tell us about this unhappiness and what you think you need to do to be happy. Are you aware of awareness? What is awareness? What is consciousness? What is your body? What is God? Who is God? Love? What are you feeling now? Now? Explain further. Where does it hurt? What happened when you were ten? Tell us about that. How? When? What do you feel now?

It sounds a lot like psychological or religious counseling, and, in a way, it is, but in another way it's not—because these counselors are speaking directly and clearly from the heart of *magic something*. They are healed. They are whole. They are happy. They are violin masters. By simply listening, watching, and being with them, I am—slowly, incrementally—absorbing their *magic something*. And that's the simple beauty of it; it's contagious. All you have to do is be in the room.

As we talk, I feel a nervous release of tension in my body, and I begin to relax . . . further and further. It's not a deep relaxation, because I'm a newbie and not very good at all this, but it's something. Eye contact with Steven and Felicia is sustained and satisfying, in a way that normal conversational eye contact *never* is. It's a profound and beautiful conversation. The hour or so quickly passes, and we conclude with another few minutes of silence.

We then say our goodbyes, and I depart. No chitchat. No promises for a future get together.

There's an unspoken and logical code of conduct in these circumstances: Don't ruin the groove you've created with unnecessary talk at the end. I slip out the door and reflect on the experience as I head to my car. One part of me is disappointed that I feel like a wet log near a fire. I can feel the fire. I can see the fire. But damn if I don't refuse to burn. It's frustrating. I want fireworks, a shift in perspective, an insight—something, damn it. The search for *magic something* seems to be littered with moments like these. On the other hand, I know that a good part of this process is downright mysterious, and I have to just trust it and shut up. Not so easily done. I get into my rental car. Time for the next teacher—Marianna.

Marianna offers the same thing on a slightly different scale. Marianna is a *very* popular *magic something* teacher. She's giving a free talk at a nearby public meeting hall. It's ten minutes away. I arrive at about ten fifteen. I'm a little late. When I walk into the hall, there are nearly three hundred people in attendance. The room has quieted down and everyone is sitting in silence. I take a seat near the back of the hall.

Marianna walks in and sits down on a cushioned seat, centered on a small stage at the front of the hall. There is a microphone on a stand, another seat—currently empty, adjacent and directly opposite hers—and between the seats, a small table with a glass of water, a bouquet of flowers, and a small framed picture of an elderly Hindu saint named Ramana Maharshi.

Marianna is in her mid-fifties, pretty and distinguished looking, with curly blondish-silver hair. She joins us in silence, eyes closed. After a few minutes, she opens her eyes and places her hands together and welcomes us . . . to satsang. This is what this church calls this meeting. It's a Sanskrit word that means "association with truth." Marianna's teacher was another Indian fellow named Papaji. Papaji's teacher was the older guy in the picture on the table. There's a long-standing tradition of *magic something* teachings passed on from one living teacher to another in India. Marianna learned and lived with one of these teachers and discovered her own *magic something* switch. Parts of her teaching are naturally reverent of this Indian tradition but only minimally. She's been pretty good at keeping her school free of a foreign or cultic vibe, and I admire her for it.

The talk begins. It's a slow, delicate discourse on the nature of doubt. A good topic, because we all know it: Doubt that the teacher is authentic. Doubt that your intentions are authentic.

Doubt that *magic something* is attainable. Doubt that you are good enough or qualified enough to actually attain it. Doubt that life will ever work out. Doubt that you'll ever be happy. The list goes on and on. It's a nice sermon—just like church—except no one is talking about a teacher who lived, spoke, and died two thousand years ago. The teacher is alive, in the room, and speaking from direct experience.

She ends her talk, then invites questions from the audience. This is the interesting part: Each questioner is asked to come up to the empty seat on the stage and, from there, ask their questions. It's to everyone's benefit. I've never done this personally and can only attest that from an audience point of view, it's a very effective method of teaching, because as you watch and listen, the questioner's fears and concerns and misgivings become your own. Sometimes the questions are great. Sometimes the questions are stupid. Marianna does not hold back her opinion or straightforward answers. In many ways, it's a dialog similar to my dialog with Steven and Felicia. It's an emotional rollercoaster ride.

It's now about eleven thirty a.m. I leave the meeting with Marianna a little early because I'm having lunch with Will Davis. I know Will, like Steven, Felicia, and Marianna, from the Internet. Will is not an official *magic something* teacher, but he is happy to share his experiences with those who ask. Will has a great website that is filled with all sorts of material about his own *magic something* journey and awakening. I like Will a lot. He's the most down-to-earth and real of the folks I'll visit today. Will turned me on to Steven and Felicia, who were his teachers.

It's about noon. Will and I meet at a Chinese restaurant in downtown San Raphael. He looks just like his website picture. Late forties, dark brown hair, goatee, well dressed. Will is a computer programmer with a day job. He's married. No kids that I know of. He's like me in the sense that he never felt the need to give up or abandon his normal life in pursuit of *magic something*. I completely respect this and easily relate to him. We talk about mundane things for a while, and eventually I begin pestering him about *magic something*. He obliges and happily answers my questions.

There aren't very many people in this world with whom you can sit down and talk about such matters, especially while eating General Tsao's chicken and egg rolls. Most teachers or mentors like these are way high on the mountain top or on stage in front of a sea of people or accessed only with a very large bank account. But here I am for the low, low cost of a buffet lunch at Ming's Oriental Express. I'm feeling pretty damn smart and pretty damn lucky.

Will and I converse for over an hour. This occasion is, of course, less intimate than my previous meetings, but it serves its purpose in that it presents my entire quest as attainable and realistic. If a guy like Will can find his *magic something*, so can I. We say goodbye. Time for the last teacher.

The day has been leading up to this. If it isn't already evident, let me be perfectly clear: I am on a serious quest to find my *magic something* switch and turn it on. I'm not putzing around. I will climb that mountain. I will walk through that desert. I will leap over that fire. I will swim with those sharks. I will sit with just about any *magic something* teacher that genuinely has something to teach—despite their quirks, crazy qualities, or off-putting styles. I'm not afraid. Nobody is too taboo or extreme for me.

This next teacher does live atop a mountain, metaphorically

bordered by a ring of fire, a vast desert, and a sea filled with man-eating sharks. He's not easy to get to. I had to jump through all manner of hoops to make this happen. I have never met this teacher in person, but I have been a student of his for nearly six years. He writes books. Lots of books. There are CDs, DVDs, workshops, weekend retreats, and levels upon levels of involvement. He has a following numbering in the thousands. He maintains retreat centers in Northern California, Hawaii, and Fiji. He is a major player on the pro *magic something* scene and has been since about 1974. If you knew nothing about these matters and bumped into him on the street, he would probably scare the hell out of you, then you'd want to give him a hug. He's a Harley Davidson ridin', two-hundred proof whiskey drinkin', hell raisin', order shoutin', *magic something* Commander-in-Chief Guru. His name is Bubba Frank, and I'm gonna hang out with him today.

It's a long drive to his literal mountain-top hermitage in the dead center of Lake County. About three hours to be exact. I drive north through a maze of windy hills, cactus scrub, coyote lookouts, and old Indian trails. These are not the days of Map-Quest or Google maps. I'm relying on state and county maps, and I'm having a hard time of it. I get lost. Ugh. I pull over to a podunk gas station, not knowing what I'm going to do or say to the attendant—*Excuse me, sir, I'm looking for Bubba Frank's Fantastical Holy Heritage and Mountain-Top Sanctuary of Bliss. Do you happen to know where that is? I'll take a Twix bar and some gas too.* Somehow, I didn't think this would fly. As luck would have it, however, I did notice a dubious-looking biker dude tanking up his bike, sporting a leather outfit, a tattoo, and a pony tail. His tattoo was a mandala, so I figured I might have a fighting chance. Instead of going through the painful process of verbalizing my desires, I simply pointed to the Bubba Frank flyer in my possession and asked. I was rewarded. He, too, was headed there and invited me to follow. Yippee. I told you, I ain't afraid of no sharks.

I follow biker Bob through a few more convoluted hillsides and winding roads. I would never have made it on my own. We arrive. In the parking lot of the sanctuary, I thank him profusely as we leave our vehicles. It's quite beautiful here. Amidst the dark conifer jungle are massive speckled-gray boulders, gravel roads, worn brown-earth walkways, ornate colorful gardens, and beautifully built brown and red buildings—all blending seamlessly into their surroundings. I take a deep breath. I'm nervous. No clue what to expect. No clue where to go. Then—the distinct sound of a conch shell being blown and the clanging of a large brass bell.

Biker Bob is still standing near me and upon hearing these sounds nearly drops his pants. I ask what all the hubbub is about, and he excitedly tells me that Bubba Frank is going to make a public appearance. He hurriedly finishes taking off his biker clothes, then rushes off. Okay. This is it.

I follow suit: Lock the car. Fix my hair. Tuck in my shirt. Run.

Where Bubba Frank is appearing is about three hundred yards down the mountain in the middle of the sanctuary. Everything is formalized here, including an occasion like this when Bubba Frank is simply walking from one location to another: from the bath-spring house to his residence. Yeah it's crazy, but this is how these folks do it. Hundreds of people begin lining up along the walkway between the two buildings. I also get in line and wait. The excitement reaches a fever pitch. The conch shell is blown again. Everyone quiets down. Bubba has left the building.

He's an old man now. Not the exuberant Bubba you'd like

him to be—from the pictures on his books or his DVDs. This is another version: Bubba in his waning years—big belly, worn face, crinkled eyes, and a cane to walk with. His hair is long, gray, and stringy. Covering him is a lengthy, flowing, orange-and-yellow robe made from light cotton. Bubba is a guru's Guru. He has no qualms about it. Take him or leave him.

As he passes down the walkway, he takes a short moment to look each person directly in the eyes. This is an Indian tradition called darshan—direct sighting of the guru. It's a touching occasion. There are a *lot* of people in the line. It's going to take him a while to get to his house. One can't help but to feel like a little kid, waiting to see Santa Claus. I'm a little nervous. I'm a little excited. Walking patiently along with him are two bodyguards and several staff members. There's something primal and archetypal about this moment. This tradition has been going on for thousands of years in India. You don't hear much about it in the West because we don't have a spiritual or religious culture that is formally oriented around such teachers or teachings. It's a completely unique occasion and worth the price of admission for no other reason.

Bubba is getting closer now. My heart pounds, and I'm getting a little lightheaded. As he approaches, I, like everyone else, kneel down and place my hands, palms spread, up in the air. I look up and face him directly. He's just a few feet and people away. Heart pounds. Knees weak. My turn. Bubba moves his head toward mine, and we lock eyes. It's a brief gaze. He seems to wince. Then—it's over. I place my hands over my heart in a formal gesture of thanks. My nerves settle down. He moves along. I return to standing. It's over and . . .

I don't know what to think. Ho-hum? Yahoo!? Yippee!? WTF? No—don't think at all. Shut up. But— Shut up, I said. All that fuss for a split-second gaze at Bubba Frank? And he winced? That's right! Two seconds? Quiet. I want my money back. You done?

I'm perplexed, a little disappointed, but mostly tired. It's been a long day. Bubba eventually finishes and enters his abode. The conch shell is blown one last time. Slowly, everyone in line scatters and leaves. I head back to my car. It's five p.m. I'm hungry. I grab a few things, then head over to the registration building. It takes a little while to register. Things like payment, food arrangements, sleeping arrangements all need to be worked out. After I'm done with this, I head over to the food hall for dinner.

The rest of the day is a bust. There's a formal evening gathering with Bubba, but I'm just too tired to attend. Well, okay, after sorting out my stuff and checking in to my lodging, despite myself, I do attend. It's a sycophantic celebratory satsang bag of crap. Bubba is on his throne with a litany of musicians, chanters, dancers, meditators, and poets all flowering him, literally and figuratively, with the gifts of their trade. Bubba's just sitting there. He says nothing. He does nothing. I guess I'm just supposed to bask and marvel in his shiny, happy presence. The occasion does nothing for me, so I leave. Not my scene. And, I'm pooped. The whole guru on a throne thing, in my opinion, has outworn its welcome. Why endure these slick overproduced theatrics when there are plenty of *magic something* teachers who'll meet you in Chinese restaurant? Sorry, Bubba. All in all, though, it's been a very good day. Instruction and teachers. I can't say I didn't give it my all. I walk to my car and drive to my overnight lodging. It's a comfortable place—if you consider a sleeping bag on the floor comfortable. Lights out. I sleep fitfully.

The next day I'm on an airplane flying home.

Water

You are water.

Frozen. Cold. Solid. Hard.

All of the other water you have ever known, your whole life, has also been frozen, cold, solid, and hard.

One day, by chance, you are told about a type of water known to be fluid, shapeless, soft, and warm. You can hardly believe it. You scoff.

Years go by.

Then, by some strange twist of fate or grace, you run into some of this water.

Fluid, shapeless, soft, and warm.

You barely recognize it—as water, that is—but somehow, you know . . . it is.

Something about this water is very appealing, very familiar, and very natural.

Simultaneously, this water offends you and frightens you.

Your world is changed.

You walk away affected.

Then, a few days later, the strangest thing happens.

You drip.

For the first time in your life . . . you drip.

You can hardly believe it.

But the drip comes and goes, and soon you forget about it.

Years go by again.

This time you see an advertisement for a gathering—with this other water.

You go.

For a full two days you sit, and listen, and watch.

You cry and laugh.

You are amazed, dumbfounded, and scared.

Never before have you had such an intense and real experience.

Now, you are really changed.

There is no going back.

No going back to believing that your true nature is frozen, cold, solid, and hard.

A few months go by.

Then, of course, the inevitable happens . . . in bucket loads.

You can't stop the dripping.

It's out of control. You are scared witless.

You are melting.

It scares you to death, because it is, in fact—indeed, your death.

Death of the frozen, cold, solid, and hard you.

Birth of the fluid, shapeless, soft, and warm you.

The melting goes on for years.

You attend other gatherings with the other water.

You melt in small drips and big drips.

Small chunks and large chunks.

It's a disconcerting and sometimes painful process.

But one day, you wake up and you realize . . .

It's done.

The frozen, cold, solid, and hard you is no more.

You didn't die.

You simply changed.

Simply returned to your true nature.

Fluid, shapeless, soft, and warm.

And now you are free . . . to flow, splash, rush, run, fall, evaporate, and return.

You are water.

I imagine that, if you picked up this book or a friend lent it to you, at some point in your life, you have dripped. Or perhaps this is your first exposure to such a topic, and your dripping has not yet begun. Maybe you've been on this course for years, and great chunks of ice regularly crash to the floor around you. Regardless of where you are on the path to discovering *magic something*, this next archetypal step is unavoidable. It's called "Walls, Blocks, and Knots." More of an ongoing process than an actual step or singular breakthrough, "Walls, Blocks, and Knots" refers to the nuts-and-bolts heart of the search for *magic something*. This is where the real work of the process is undergone; where the grease hits the axle, the tread the road, the oil the piston, the sandpaper the block. This is where you confront your fears, limitations, and resistances. This is where you drip, crack, and melt. Without this step, no human being would ever transform and arrive at the *magic something* summit. This is your chance to be the hero, and the only person you have to save . . . is yourself.

Archetypal Step 5: Walls, Blocks, and Knots

"During the drive home, I realize . . . this will not be the end of it. This was the biggest encounter I've ever had with this beast, but it will be back. This I'm sure of. *At least*, I think to myself, *when it does come back, I will be able to handle it. I will have the courage to handle it. Yes I will.*"

Two years later: It's seven a.m., February 6, 1999.

I'm sick. Ugh. I have a terrible cough, and I need some cough medicine. Only I don't have any cough medicine, *and*—much worse—I don't have any cash. Sounds like an easy problem to remedy; I know—ATM machine—but A) I have no money in my account, B) my bank has no local ATM machine, and C) my bank is a half an hour away. The only thing I *do* have are several checks made out to the business I run. It's a small amount of money, but enough, certainly, to get the goods. All I have to do is drag my sorry ass out of bed, walk through the freezing cold, get into my car, and drive down the road. Not a thrilling prospect.

As I'm pondering this immensely inane situation, I have another coughing attack which serves as a cattle prod to stir my lazy and sickly bovine existence into action. I am now resolute in my determination to make the dreaded trip.

I quickly get dressed, bundle up, and walk out to the car. No sign of roommates—too early for them. I get in my car, start it up, and peel down the driveway.

I room with another guy and two girls. We're all around the same age. I'll be thirty this year. We live in an old farmhouse surrounded by about three hundred acres of state-designated park. Nice place to live. It's called Skylark Farm. We all love it and treat it like our own, even though we're just renters. I've been living here for about four years. I'm self-employed. My company is called Sealife Aquarium Service. I've been cleaning fish tanks for about five years. I hate it; primarily because I'm tired of slopping up fish shit; secondarily because I'm in the midst of negotiating the sale of the company, and I have one foot out the door; and lastly because about four months ago, I received a very partial grant to produce a big rock musical I wrote called *Magic Music Myth*, and I'd *much* rather be pursuing this. I am stewing a fetid pot of possibility, desire, ambition, hope, and fear. I have a lot on my mind.

Most of what's on my mind, however, plays a depressing second fiddle to my coughing and hacking. I make my way down a cold, misty, gray, and bleak highway. It's a torturous half-hour drive to the bank. My mind spins into delirium.

Getting closer. Sucks. Heavy heart. *Who am I? Witness?* Almost. . . . Bank. *What am I doing?* Feel like I'm in a bubble two thousand miles away. *Who? Witnessing.* If I . . . sell business . . . don't get rest of grant money. Show. Screwed. *Witnessing? Yes.* Will have to get job. Just sell the damn business. Finally. Bank. Irritation, chest. Cough. Headache. Drive up window. Teller there. Thank god. *Who am I?* Roll window down. Hi. Morning. Cough. Checks, tube. Push button. Cash these please. *Who!* . . . *Who am I?* Hold back cough. Roll up window. Headachy. Tired. Lot to do. Send out more faxes. *Witness.* Other aquarium services. *Is that who I am?* Hack. Hack. Come on. Money now, please. *Awareness.* Okay. Send it. Send it. Send it. What's the holdup? Cough. Cover mouth. Finally. Here comes. *Who?* . . . Roll down window. Take tube. Thanks. *Am I the witness?* Drive.

I speed out of the bank parking lot in a condition that would probably qualify me for a DUI, but luckily it's early Saturday morning—there's no fuzz around. I wind my way *back* down the road, coughing and stammering all the way. I drive to the local Walmart, enter, and make my way to the pharmacy section.

Grab the goods. Cough syrup. Hold back cough. *Again . . . Who am I? The Witness.* Checkout counter. One person ahead of me. Cough. Hand over mouth. Slightly dizzy. What's the holdup? Let's go. Let's go. *Awareness. Feel like I'm in a Bubble.* Register broken. Okay, another register? Only one open. Got to be shitting me. Ugh. Come on! Damn it. *Witnessing.* Fuck this. Drop goods. Cough. Pissed off. Leave. *Witness . . .* Angry. *Am I really angry?* Walk to car. Start engine. *No, not really. I'm witnessing the anger.* Hack. Cough. Zip out of parking lot. Giant pharmacy just up block. Drive. Delirious. *Witness?* Arrive. Cough. Get out of car. Walk. Inside. Pharmacy section? Pharmacy? Got it. Walk. Grab goods. Cough syrup. *Who am I?* The hell with it. Open bottle now. Chug. Ahhh—yuck! Terrible shit. Register. Pay. Leave. *Witness? Delirium. In a bubble.* Cough. Drive home.

It's a quick, five-minute drive home. I pull into the driveway and, like a zombie, walk back into the house and up to my room. I'm the living dead. I lie down on my bed. I'm in a very strange space. I'm ripe for the universe to turn me inside out. I'm ripe for a *very* large chunk of ice to melt off, fall, and crush my existence into pieces. I'm ripe to meet the anti-maker. I'm ripe to meet FEAR. FEAR itself. Existential FEAR. The beast of all FEARS.

I wake up an hour or so later plagued by Sealife Aquarium Service and *Magic Music Myth* thoughts. I walk out to my office to do some paperwork. Send some faxes. Pay some bills. Worry. Stress. Contrive. Control. Last-ditch efforts to make something of my life.

It's coming, but I can't see it coming. It's good that it's a surprise. I would never go willingly. No one would. I'm an oblivious idiot puppet plaything, flitting in the wind of God's mercurial mind. I'm a discarded no-name object-thing. I'm a dusty worn out toy about to be recycled. I work for several hours in my office. Late in the day now. The coughing returns. Time to chug some more medicine. And I do. It's a mistake. A good mistake. A very bad mistake.

I'm already in a disconnected, filmy, vague, discombobulated state, and the cough medicine adds no clarity. It takes me deeper into my hole. Primordial deep. Dark. Heavy. Black. Deep. I leave the office. *I am the witness.* I float over to the house. My roommate is in the kitchen. *Witness.* I talk with her. *There is no Jeff talking. There's only the experience of talking. I am identified only as the witness. I am no longer Jeff. I am the witness experiencing Jeff.* We talk. Pretend—like there is something important to say. Then . . .

Hello, Beast. My brain, heart, and body ignite with a fire of FEAR. DEATH. *Now. Die. No avoiding it this time.* The fear rumbles across my existence like a nuclear rocket down a dirt road. It looms on the horizon. I hear it coming for me. I politely leave my roommate. I walk upstairs to my bedroom. The FEAR rips apart my will, my efforts, my dreams, my control. It threatens to explode my life into a million pieces. *I will let it. I am nobody. I am a dead man walking. Annihilate me.* The full brunt of the nuclear explosion has yet to occur. I sit down on the bed. I gaze at the electrical outlet on the opposite wall. I take a deep breath. *I am the Witness. I can handle this. Come now. Take me.* It does.

I enter a space of fear beyond all imagination. I am seated in the center of a nuclear explosion. My heart pounds fiercely.

Energy pours out my hands, lips, feet, and the top of my head—
literal electrical voltage-like energy—at the speed of light. I am
rattled to my utmost core. Nervous. Shaking. Wide eyed. Every
atom in my body feels as if it flips polarity. Every cell relaxes.
Every muscle loosens. I die a thousand deaths. The release is
beyond knowing, beyond bliss. It is acceptance—the final acceptance of loss. Loss of self. Loss of identity with self. *I am the Witness now. I am the Consciousness behind all life. This is who I am.*
It ends. It has passed. It is *finally* over. No more running. No
more hiding. Wall torn down. Block removed. Knot undone. I
am free.

The Mountain and the River

Before *magic something,* you suffer from all sorts of delusions about who you think you are and what you think life is all about. Mountains are mountains, rivers are rivers, and nothing is right in the world. During the blossoming of *magic something,* you delight in all sorts of blissful delusions about who you think you are and what you think life is all about. Mountains become rivers, rivers become mountains, and only sometimes are things right in the world. After *magic something,* you know who you are and are happy not understanding what life is all about. Mountains go back to being mountains, rivers go back to being rivers, and everything is just right in the world.

It's six a.m. I'm up making coffee, and I'm making a colossal mess of it because I don't know where a damn thing is. This isn't my kitchen.

We're at my parents' place in the country. Elisabeth, Jeremy, and I traveled out here yesterday afternoon. It's a two-hour jaunt from our place—a short distance for a simple getaway weekend or, as my family refers to it, a poor man's vacation. Call it whatever—it's a welcomed change of scenery. Nuttin' much planned. We may go visit my high school. Elisabeth's never been, and I haven't seen it myself in over a decade. I may go fishin' with my

Pop. I bought him a fly rod outfit for Father's Day this year and have been torturing him with it ever since. (He's not the fishing fanatic I am.) Other than that, I plan to sedate myself with beer, couch, and television. Elisabeth and I don't have cable TV, just a DVD player, so when we visit my parents, I transmogrify into a spud-like creature with remote controls sprouting out of my head and beer bottles affixed to my lips and hands. It's quite gratifying. I never said *magic something* turned you into a sophisticate.

A few hours later, everyone is up. My Mom and Elisabeth announce that they are going to a yoga class. Jeremy's mine for the morning. Everyone goes their separate ways. Jeremy and I are left standing in the kitchen. Well. No beer and television yet. I tell Jeremy that it's horsey-feeding time. He gets excited as punch at this announcement, and we go about preparing the necessary victuals: apples and carrots. We garner a healthy-sized bag and are off. It's a short walk down to the field where the neighbor's horses reside.

A few minutes later we arrive. The horses have accommodated our excursion. Both horses are out—lollygagging in their verdant expanse. They see us. We see them. The game is on. Jeremy and I walk up to the paltry electric fence which separates their world from ours. They march over to us. I don't know jack about horses, but I think these are . . . uh . . . mares or guys. Both are coffee-latte brown. One appears to be older than the other. The younger one is about a foot taller than the older one. They seem to be super friendly, but I suppose anybody proffering edible gifts would elicit this behavior from them. I apprehensively admire their very large, ugly, yellow teeth juxtaposed with Jeremy's tiny fingers. I show Jeremy the proper way to deliver the goods—palms flat, fingers closed. Jeremy enjoys the whole show and eagerly hands over the contents of our bag. The horses happily oblige, and in a few short minutes, the victuals have disappeared down their gullets.

In this moment, I don't really have anything to report about *magic something*. There is no *magic something* standing out against anything else. I'm knee deep in normality. It's the weekend. I'm on family time. Everything is a-okay just as it is. Perhaps there's a native intelligence within *magic something* that recognizes its own necessity. It's a mystery to me. Right now, I feel fine, happy, and content, and there's no need for fireworks. I know this. Maybe *magic something* knows this. We both agree. Mountains are mountains and horses are horses.

The hours tick away. Jeremy and I return to the house and have some indoor playtime. My Mom and Elisabeth return from yoga. They shower and get dressed and prepare for their next outing, this time with Jeremy, to the local grocery store and town shopping center. I'm left to my own low-key devices. I have the afternoon to myself and slowly turn into the aforementioned potato creature. I do a little reading, television watching, and take a nap.

Everyone returns around two p.m. The *magic something* fireworks return around this time as well. I guess its native intelligence knows that something is afoot—and it is: We're going to visit my high school this afternoon. Gulp. It's been nearly ten years since I set foot on the grounds. I'm nervous. I admit, this is a somewhat contrived expedition, but I also see it as exploratory research to find out how *magic something* reacts and responds in the face of important or serious experiences from a person's past. (I pretty much know the answer to this and what the outcome will be, but thought you'd like to see for yourself.)

Imagine taking a flashlight into your attic, which you haven't visited for ten years, and seeing all sorts of cobwebs, creepy-crawlies, and monsters. You're going to want to clean 'em up and kick 'em out. Not that I had any creepy-crawly or tragic experiences in high school; I just suffered, probably like you, the normal litany of teenage insecurities. It's a minor thing, I know. But this is a good example of one strange facet of *magic something:* It compels you to be absolutely thorough. Have you been or are you currently avoiding any fears, insecurities, or anxieties? Yes? Go get your flashlight. You've got some cleanin' to do.

I went to a private Episcopalian boarding school located about thirty minutes from my parents' place. I boarded there for two years when I was in the eighth and ninth grades, then, when I got my driver's license, I became a day student. I was a day student until I graduated. The school is situated on about a hundred and fifty rolling acres in the rural countryside of western Maryland. The grounds look like a miniature college campus: old brick buildings festooned with ivy, a small chapel, dormitories, gymnasium, library, infirmary, dining hall, plenty of large old oak trees, a pond, sports fields everywhere, and sidewalks gently connecting the whole. It was a self-contained little island of college-preparatory academia. It wasn't perfect; there were very few girls attending, sports were stressed too much, music and arts weren't stressed enough, and we had to attend chapel every day. I had my ups and downs with the school, but by and large had a good experience there. I'm a proud alumnus.

I graduated in 1987 and returned a few times while I was in college and maybe once when I was in my late twenties, but I haven't been back in over ten years. Things have changed—a lot of things, I'm about to find out. A bowling ball grows in my stomach as Elisabeth, Jeremy, and I retrace the route I drove hundreds of times as a teenager. It's a single lane, tree-lined, tight, rolling, curvy, and dangerous road. I point out to Elisabeth a dented spot in an old rock wall where I had my first car wreck. *Magic something* amps up to maximum. I'm glad Elisabeth's driving. I'm all befuddled. In just over thirty minutes, we arrive. I should remind you that today is Saturday, so I'm not expecting the campus to be in full bustle mode. However, it would be nice to see somebody. I'm hoping a few students or staff members will be around. We pull into the main entrance and cruise down to the parking lot, and, yep, there's my old space.

What the hell. We park in it. Jitters. Nerves. *Magic something*. Deep breath. Get out of the car. Jeremy's asleep. Pick him up. Sling him over my shoulder. Gather nerves. Think: The last time I was here, I most definitely did not have spawn. I didn't have a wife either, actually. And . . . I definitely didn't have *magic something*. Damn I've changed; and the campus has also really changed—for the better. I'm impressed. It's beautiful.

Okay, now before I go on, let's talk about *magic something*, because at this juncture the one thing that I knew was going to happen has just happened, and you should know about it. The attic full of creepy-crawlies has been cleaned out. The jitters, the nervousness, the bowling ball in my stomach are gone—happened when I stepped out of the car. It was simply a matter of allowing, accepting, and confronting. This process occurs time and time again when searching for and living with *magic something*. Today's incident is paltry compared to my report in "Walls, Blocks, and Knots" of day 15, but it is worth noting because it demonstrates how our whole being utilizes *magic something* to do ongoing house cleaning.

Life is, at it's most basic biological level, tension. It's natural. What isn't natural (well, maybe it's natural but not comfortable) is accumulating and carrying excessive amounts of this tension throughout our whole lives. Everyone collects tension "baggage" in the form of stress, anxiety, and fear. Discovering and living with *magic something* is very much about removing this tension. Not all of it. You can never remove all of it. But you can remove most of it. Discovering and living with *magic something* is about returning to your body's natural level of tension, which, as reported in this book, can be quite pleasurable, but only if you're willing to step through the fire first. In other words, avoiding the creepy-crawlies in your attic is a bad idea.

I feel fine now; the self-assured, pleasurable, and grounded quality of *magic something* has returned. Before this small transition, I was a nervous student returning to his old high school. Now I'm just a nobody tourist and free to explore the campus as I see fit. So we do.

Jeremy is still asleep slung over my shoulder. As we walk toward the center of the campus, he wakes up and beckons for Mama. Elisabeth takes him. We walk on stepping stones lying between (what was once) the infirmary and the main building—a path I walked many, many times oh so long ago. We arrive at the center of the campus. There are multiple brick buildings all surrounding a huge circular driveway, at the center of which is a large island of green grass. There's a new, tastefully sized and crafted brick wall that surrounds the edge of the grass island. In the center of the island still stands one of the largest oak trees on the campus. Who knows how old it is. It's a venerable old oak, held up with steel cables that imbue it with an ancient, crotchety, wizened feel.

The campus is mostly empty of people. There are some students, a guy and two girls, hanging out on the new circular brick wall. We ask if any of the buildings are open. Nope. Most are locked on the weekends. We chitchat a bit, then continue our walk. Two adults appear from the infirmary, and we introduce ourselves to them. They've got keys! They'll happily unlock the chapel and the main schoolhouse. We head to the schoolhouse first. It's now twice the size it used to be. We peek around. All my old classrooms are still intact. The library used to be a part of this building. It's now been moved to its own separate building. Nice. The main schoolhouse is in great shape—strong, vibrant, and clear. It's grown. It's changed with the times. It's modern and up to date. Very nice. It's warm and inviting. It retains an efficient elegance that clearly says that this building is a topnotch place to receive an education. That's private school for you. Then, sigh, we move on to the chapel . . .

Oh, the chapel. What a sad, empty, dry, little chapel it was when I was a student here, and now, it's exactly the same. It's a perfect example of what happens to a human being, an institution, a creed, belief, or religion . . . when the creepy-crawlies aren't cleaned from the attic. It becomes clogged, stuck, and stagnant—a mere symbol of something long ago, long forgotten, and long dead. Nothing about it shouts *now*. And certainly nothing about it shouts *magic something*.

My own *magic something* is well on as we walk inside, and I am hoping for the best. But as we enter, I am struck with sad disappointment. It looks the same. It feels the same. Empty—and not just of people; there's no trace of *magic something* in this building. I would feel it. Probably never was. It's no wonder that I graduated from this school a professed agnostic/atheist. All I want to do is get out. There is nothing for me here. Never was. Too bad. Honestly, I half expected it. This is a private, college preparatory school, not a seminary or zen-dō. Oh, well.

We leave and meander around more of the campus. There are many new buildings that I don't recognize. New walkways. New nooks and crannies. New outdoor spaces. One of them is a very lovely outdoor seating area, adorned with large, handmade wooden furniture and a small fountain with reflecting pool. It's a great detail. Aha! Here is some life! The flowing water, the natural wood, the rock patio—all natural elements built into a usable, sociable outdoor space. We sit for a moment and take it in. This little addition probably impresses me the most. It's got charm, which means it's got heart, which means, of course, it's got *magic something*. The person who donated this little outdoor feature obviously knew this, because on a plaque above the fountain is the following inscription:

> *"Education is vital, but make sure that your heart
> expands faster than your mind."*
> —James Montgomery Schurz

There's hope for my old school after all. We continue our walk. I guide Elisabeth and Jeremy around the back of the main building and down to another water feature: the campus spring-fed pond. From a distance, it's a beautiful little pond—complete with statues, walking paths, an island, and a bridge. But as we get closer, it's evident that the pond has some major issues. It's completely silted in for starters, maybe three feet deep at best. There are no fish and no signs of other wildlife—tiny or large—either. It's another campus dead zone.

Okay, before I launch into a *magic something* ecological diatribe, I will say this: I am a complete nature Nazi. Leave nature alone. Or, if you mess with nature, at least have the decency to do it in a way that has minimal impact on it and/or naturally supports it. I'm an outdoor nutcase. What can I say? The connection between nature and *magic something* is so obvious I won't even bother. My old school is a perfect example of the modern world: intelligent to a limit, smart above average, and in dire need of some basic lessons about *magic something*, the natural world, and whole living. There's no balance. I'm not picketing for a flower-power revolution here. Just balance.

Jeremy is getting hungry and antsy. Time to wrap up our visit. It's been nice. I want to see more. My judgments have been based on an empty campus and the inside of two buildings. Not really fair. I'll be back. I'm glad we came. Glad to proudly show off my old school to Jeremy and Elisabeth. Glad to visit my old stomping grounds. Glad to take it all in through the blessed lens of *magic something*.

We head back home via the same route we came. Upon returning, we prepare to go out to eat with Grandpa and Grandma. We all drive over to a small college town in West Virginia and have dinner with some friends at a Thai restaurant. It's nice but a little frustrating with Jeremy. It's hard to dine at a nice restaurant with a three-year-old in tow. It's been a long day for him. I understand, but I also know I'll be paying big bucks for this dinner and want to enjoy it. His breakdown during the main course doesn't make this possible. Ugh. Oh, well. Too much in one day. We scurry out the door and drive back home. He falls asleep in transit. We arrive at Grandma and Grandpa's. Everyone crawls into their beds. It's been a good day.

The Seeker and the Fly Fisherman

If you are already a seeker of
magic something, this day is for you.
If you are a fly fisherman,
this day is for you, too.

It's Sunday, six thirty a.m. I'm up and show a slight improvement in my foreign kitchen–navigation skills. I putz around with
coffee and breakfast until Jeremy comes down. He steals a few
bites of my toast, then we read books and play with toys until
everyone else gets up. I partake in breakfast part two, then prepare for the real event of the day: Dad and I are heading off to
church. The church is called Beaver Creek. The form of prayer is
called fly-fishing. What we pray for is big, fat rainbow trout on
the end of our lines.

The sermon this day is titled "Disappointment," and it's for
anyone who has ever sincerely embarked upon the adventure of
seeking *magic something.* I say *sincerely* because to understand this
type of disappointment, you need to have made some progress
in the *magic something* adventure. To be clear: Disappointment
is not one of the archetypal steps. It's just a general, overall term,
descriptive of the many got it/lost it moments that litter the path

throughout the search. Disappointment is to *magic something* as catching fish is to fly-fishing.

Dad and I arrive at the parking lot of the designated Beaver Creek catch-and-release, fly-fishing-only section. We park the car on a grassy knoll, get out, and gear up. My anticipation is boiling like an overdue volcano. I'm having visions of a giant, sow-sized trout bending my rod to breaking point and a photograph of me with my prized pig-fish on the cover of *Fly Fisherman* magazine. My boots are on. My rod is in hand. Requisite gear is strapped to my waist. Irresistible, imitation black-ant fly is double-clinch knotted to the tippet portion of my line. Ditto for my dad. We hop on to a neatly manicured path, which rolls merrily through some bucolic woods down to the creek.

"Philosophical Disappointment" is probably a better name for this sermon, because it refers to life, not the Playstation 3 you pined for and didn't get on your thirty-fifth birthday. Long-time *magic something* seekers are quite familiar with philosophical disappointment. It goes something like this: No matter how many breakthroughs you've had or revelations you've received or mind-blowing experiences you've attained, you are always left with a subtle to not-so-subtle feeling of disappointment. Worse, you might have had an extended days- or weeks-long visit into the *magic something* kingdom, only to be harshly dropped back into your previous miserable existence. You never seem to arrive at a point where disappointment has been completely and forever eradicated. You never seem to catch *all* of the big fish.

My dad and I walk down the last leg of the path, and I can now see the promised land. It's a small, tree-lined, limestone, spring-fed creek. Clear as vodka. (Why do all the fishing magazines say *gin*?) It's about ten to twenty feet wide and anywhere from a few inches to several feet deep. It's a total technical night-mare. I'll need to cast among the trees using a technique called roll cast, which I suck at but am willing to put up with because the fish/carrot dangling on the string in front of me is a big one: rainbow trout, brown trout, bigguns. I hooked into one this past summer, so I know they're here. Never landed it. I've been wait-ing ever since—silently, patiently—for my victorious return.

The reason disappointment piles up mountainously high on the *magic something* path is quite elementary: too much expec-tation. Expectation levels are always too high. This is pretty normal. Here's why: It's biological. It's psychological. You are a walking-talking-living-breathing *more* machine. The human mind, or ego as the term is used in *magic something* circles, is a very complex processing machine, built upon one very simple process: *more please.* Enough is never enough. More is desired. More is sought. More is a thirst never sated. More. More. More. I suppose it's a survival thing. I suppose it's natural. The problem, however, is that most people's sense of self, well-being, and hap-piness rely heavily on the results of the more machine. It's a pre-dicament that causes most human beings all sorts of suffering.

I begin my frenzied roll-casting attempts into the first pool. Dad watches. He was here with me the last time, so also knows of the big fish in these waters. No love in this pool. We begin walk-ing upstream. More attempts. More snubbing and ignoring. Not a bite or sign of fish . . . damn it. About this time, another angler with a big, professional-sized camera draped over his shoul-der walks our way. We exchange the perfunctory fly fisherman greeting: *Any luck?* Nope. He admits, however, that his was more of a photographic expedition. Cool, he hasn't spooked all the big monster fish that are waiting for me upstream. Dad lingers and chats. I'm not feeling chatty, so I continue walking and roll casting. Then, thank god, circumstances get better. I'm still not catching fish, but something else dramatically improves: The woods clear out a bit, and I can cast *for real* now—long looped casts requiring my whole body; my whole concentration. This is one of the cures to fly-fishing disappointment. Casting done well—the rhythm, the movement, the dance—is bliss; add to that a fish on the line, and you have an adrenaline-induced state of perfection. But you can't always rely on the fish, you have to fall back into the entire experience.

A *magic something* seeker is like a hospital patient with a broken leg, who, upon being healed and released from the hospital, expects to be an Olympic gymnast capable of levitation. No, stupid. You *expect* too much. It was just a broken leg. When you become grateful to *just* be healed of your broken leg, then you will have found the true essence of *magic something.* You don't become superman. You become supernormal, resting comfortably in the *total normal experience.* Then, yes, magical things begin to happen, which, of course, naturally come and go. But to arrive at this point, you must get your expectations in proper order: normal first; magic second.

It takes a *long* time to appreciate every nuance of fly-fishing, especially the point at which you actually don't care if you catch fish: The fish becomes the cherry on top. Today, for instance, I loved preparing, driving, gearing up, and executing this whole adventure. Flies must be selected. Locations must be scouted. Times allotted. Equipment gathered and fussed over, etc. I love it all.

This helps when you're in the predicament I'm in: still zero on the fish-catching front. I hop from pool to pool, switching flies several times, throwing in sticks of dynamite from time to time. Nothing works. Dad eventually joins me. We can even see the fish now, schools of them, resting on the pebble-stone stream bottom. I try beaded, weighted nymph flies that get down to them. Nuttin'. No response. Ugh. They win. Just one more cast . . .

I want to be clear on an important point pertinent to the *magic something* seeker during these times of disappointment: You can never be rid of your "more-please" mind. Got it? Ego remains. It's fantasy and fallacy to think that you can rid yourself of ego. To function as a normal human being, you absolutely need your egoic, more-please mind. Without it, you wouldn't get out of bed in the morning or realize that watching game shows on television all day long is a bad thing. What you *can* do is transcend it, which means you witness it from a distance and no longer take it seriously; but you will never live in a permanent state of egoless bliss. Realizing this is a real lesson in acceptance: Life is disappointing. Life even with *magic something* is disappointing. But this is okay, because periodically, as evidenced by the chronicles in this book, you do indeed catch fish; sometimes, even big ones. But best of all, you learn to simply enjoy the entire art of fishing.

Today is not my day to catch fish at Beaver Creek. Dad and I decide to pack it up and begin our trek back to the car. I've heard of other fisherman who didn't catch fish here, or figure out how to catch fish here, until the fourth or fifth visit. Three more visits to go, I guess. That's fishin'. Love it or leave it. I choose to love it, even on non-fish-catchin' days. Shoot, everybody knows a bad day fishin' is better than a good day workin'.

Dad and I meander back home. We stop for lunch at a small barbecue place. Next to it is a vegetable stand. I go shopping while the sandwiches are being made. I purchase a big ol' fat pumpkin for Jeremy. We eat, then drive back home.

We arrive, and the day slowly slips into late afternoon. Elisabeth and I make plans to visit some family friends and their outdoor hot tub. Grandma and Grandpa assume Jeremy duty. I slip into full *magic something* regalia for some strange reason and a hot tubbin' we go. It's a pleasant break. The cool air wafts over us as we sit in a big bowl of steaming hot water. I melt into the pretty vista filled with my old friends the Blue Ridge Mountains. At the risk of becoming human prunes, we finally, begrudgingly, exit our watery haven. Afterward, we hang around a little longer, drink beer, and chitchat with our friends. It's a nice time, but I'm eager to be off, and this is when Roger (not his real name) offers to give me a ride home . . . in his fully operational, road-worthy and licensed, candy-apple red, 1937 Chevy fire truck. Yahoo! Hell yes! Now that sounds like a hoot! One odd, unique, and charming experience coming right up! And damn if there wasn't a small *magic something* lesson nestled right in the middle of it.

Like I am a lover of fly-fishing, Roger is a lover of fire engines and trains. I feel sorry for people who don't harbor a passion for something. Nothing beats the feeling of your heart dancing a jig to the beat of something you love—doesn't matter what it is: rock climbing, line dancing, computer building, motorcycle maintenance, hot air ballooning, or stamp collecting. Passions are accompanied by a throng of mutual benefits and enterprises: friends, community, creativity, problem solving, travel, adventure, education, team building, soul building . . . the list goes on.

I'm about to get a good dose of Roger's passion. I'm happy to do so. It's an open-topped fire engine, with wheels that look like they belong on a mountain bike, a water-holding tank not much bigger than my old fish tank, and a combo hose and ladder unit that I wouldn't trust to dowse my grill or gain access to my front-porch roof. The truck's about twenty feet long. Four gears. No clutch. No seat belts. It's awesome.

I hop in the passenger side, and Roger pushes the button that ignites the confibulator, which rotates the starter, which fires the thruster, which does the two-step that coughs the old engine to life. Works like a charm. Sounds just like you'd expect—clanky, gurgling, loud, and rough; a sound assuring you that this old rust bucket can still get down to business. At a top speed of forty miles per hour, this little fire engine is all heart. We pull out of Roger's driveway, wind blowing in my face. It's great. We turn onto a small country road, twist down a few hills, and then arrive at the two-lane interstate. Yep, it's legal. Old red's got tags. We pull onto the interstate, and Roger gives it all it's got. It's really loud now. Roger and I have to yell to hear one another. Bugs are zooming by my head at what seems to be Mach 7. Did I mention there's no side doors? Oh, hell yes!! No pansy-ass seatbelts or doors on this baby! We cruise down the road, and I am all smiles. Roger's passion is infectious. I'm blown into wide open *magic something*. My hat is nearly blown off my head. Nothing could be better than this odd little moment.

Roger decides to take a detour through a small town. We exit the interstate. Gear down. Bugs zoom slightly slower. We weave our way through the town, and this is when the *magic something* lesson hits me: As we cross through the main section of town, everybody waves and smiles at us. We wave and smile back. It's funnier than hell, and everybody joins us in the mini-parade. Now, I'm not pooh-poohing this experience in any way, but *magic something* shouts the obvious: How odd it is that it takes two thousand pounds of red-painted steel affixed to four wheels, a hose, a ladder, and a water tank to make strangers smile, laugh, and wave to one another. It's happiness—dependent upon conditions. Not that there's anything wrong with conditions. I love conditions. Passions are conditions. I have many passions. But I hold them in the proper context. No passion is a substitute for *magic something*. No love for something is bigger than love itself. It's a simple lesson: *Magic something* transcends conditions and passions. *Magic something* transcends fire engines; *magic something* transcends fly-fishing.

We jump back onto the interstate and plod on toward my parents' house. We arrive and before parking, honk the horn, which definitely sounds like a horn attached to something unusual. Mom, Dad, Jeremy, and Elisabeth all come bounding out of the house. Jeremy is wide eyed with surprise. We pose for a few photographs, smiling, laughing all the while. Jeremy eventually gets his fill. I thank Roger for the lift. I thank him for the fun and retire inside.

It's been a good, long, full day and weekend. We all eat dinner, then Elisabeth and I begin packing the car. Driving back home at night is easier than a morning commute. We say goodbye to Grandma and Grandpa and are off. It's a two-and-a-half-hour drive home. Jeremy sleeps through most of it. Elisabeth and I share the driving. We arrive late, unpack, and, exhausted, go to bed.

The Dragon

Everyone knows that dragons do not exist.

Mention a dragon to a Wall Street financier, and, for your efforts, you will get a face full of scoff. Everyone knows that dragons *have never* existed.

Mention dragons to a scientist, and he will reply: "Have they ever dug up dragon bones?"

Everyone knows that dragons *could never* have existed.

Mention dragons to an aeronautical engineer, and he will howl. Mention dragons to a firefighter, and he will raise his eyebrows in indulgent disdain.

Everyone knows that dragons are pure fiction, created by man to explain the unexplainable, frighten little children at bedtime, and entertain us in our boredom.

Everyone knows that dragons do not exist.

But, you see, I am not everyone.

The journey I have taken is not for everyone.

The journey I have completed is not for everyone.

Take this journey, and you will see . . .

There are indeed dragons.

Dragons you must kill.

Dragons you must capture.

Dragons you must tame.

Dragons you must ride.

Dragons you must love.

The real dragon, the one that truly does exist, is an awakening to a part of yourself that, prior to the awakening, you could never have imagined existed.

Everyone knows that dragons do not exist.

How about you?

It's four thirty. Jeremy is up *very* early. We go downstairs. I make an agreement with him: He will play quietly with his toys, while I write on my computer. He agrees. This lasts until about six, then our normal morning routine unfolds. Today you and I will part ways; I have to go to work in a few hours. You stay and read about the sixth archetypal step.

Contrary to what you may think or believe, the awakening of *magic something* is a very messy biological, psychological, and emotional process. The myth of neat, clean, instant, and permanent realization of *magic something* can be thrown into the garbage heap and incinerated. There is a great scene in the movie *Avatar* in which the hero has to capture, tame, and ride a dragon to prove himself worthy to the natives. He goes through an incredible gauntlet to accomplish this feat. This is what it's like to finally discover *magic something*. No matter what you may think or believe about riding dragons, you really have no clue until you actually ride one. I didn't.

Archetypal Step 6: Discovery and Breakthrough

It's three a.m., Thursday, September 2, 2004. I'm up. Ugh. Sleepless night again. Either I'm in the birth canal of *magic some-*

thing, or I slipped and fell into the washing machine. Can't tell. I think—pretty sure—I've been going in and out of *magic something* for five days now. Tired. Stressed. Amazed. Astounded. Discombobulated. Is this really happening? I'm lying in bed at our farmhouse in Maryland. Elisabeth is in Austria visiting her family and has been gone since Monday, the day after the first tremors of the awakening began. What started out as a slight ground shaking will culminate at about nine thirty tonight in a full-fledged 9.0 earthquake. It's going to be a long day.

This whole process began on Sunday while Elisabeth and I were, of all the places, in a swimming quarry in West Virginia, out near my parents' place. It's a *very* deep quarry. I'd been swimming there on many other occasions, so there was nothing new about it, except that something felt really wrong. I couldn't put my finger on it—I just felt creeped out by the quarry that day, like someone had just died there or, worse, had been murdered there; or a scaly leviathan from the depths was about to surface and yank us both back to its lair; or a top-secret, underwater, government UFO laboratory was hidden in the murky depths below our dangling feet. Whatever the circumstance, I felt like we were about to be in *big* trouble. Something was wrong—just not with the quarry.

We drove back to my parents' place, and a few hours later is when it happened: the first actual stirring of spontaneous *magic something,* right in the middle of dinner, of all times. It felt like a slight tickle in my heart, which then expanded to my head and brain. In about thirty seconds, I shifted to a hyper-aware, deeply relaxed state that normally would take me about thirty minutes to achieve, and then only if in the company of a *magic something* teacher. Giddy and discombobulated, I excused myself from dinner. Since that time (about five days now), it's been coming and going with varying strength and duration.

Four a.m. I have to work today, and the job I've scheduled is far away and too early. I'm stressed about the logistics of getting there on time and spending the whole day there in my current state, which is a madhouse of emotional ups and downs. I lie in bed mulling it over until about five, then get up and bite the bullet. I don't want to go, but I have a commitment to keep. I make coffee, then pack my tools. Check the map. Leave. It's a long drive through back-county roads. I make it to the river and cross it. *Is this the right road? Ugh.* Stop the car. Look at the map. *Where the hell am I? Ugh. Lost.* My anxiety and frustration mount. Everything screams at me to turn around and go back home. I call my customer. *No cell service. Arrgh! I cannot work today— not in this state! What is happening to me?!* I listen to the screaming. I turn the car around. Agitated. Tired. *I'll call in sick. Can't do this. The hell with it.* I drive back home. *Lack of sleep—that's part of it. But the hazy disorienting magic something fog? Ugh. Definitely not as advertised.* I arrive home and flop back into bed. I sleep fitfully but manage to catch up on a few hours.

Nine a.m. I get out of bed. I feel like I'm on planet Zircon in the fifth dimension somewhere in a galaxy far, far away. A hazy version of *magic something* is back. *Definitely glad I'm not using power tools.* I go and do some office work. Call the customer. Leave a message: Feel sick today; too far out of my service area; try this company; bye. Pay a few bills. *Still hazy, but different, expanded . . .* I need a few things from Staples and Target, so I hop into my car again. *Strange. Where's my concentration?* I drive by the bank first, then head over to Staples. I'm in Staples for about a minute: *Oh . . . My . . . God . . . what is this?* It's my first experience of grocery store *magic something*—an unfocused, dizzying *magic something*. Not reigned in. Not fully born. Not fully developed. I can barely stand, much less remember what I'm shopping for. *Holy crap, this is some serious shit. Is this magic something?* I manage to remember why I'm there, make the purchase, then leave. I head over to Target for more punishment. Same thing there, but, because I expect it, this time I enjoy it a little. It soon wears me down. Too much energy. Too much stimulation. I leave and scuttle back to the farm.

Noon. I still feel like I'm floating high above the earth and have about half my brain to work with. I'm worthless for every other enterprise except watching TV, normally an anathema to me on a sunny Saturday afternoon. Screw it. TV on. DVD player on. Plop my ass on the floor in front of the sofa. I decide to watch an old Bubba Frank (*magic something* teacher) DVD. I play it for about three minutes and vehemently lose interest. *Not what I need. Okay what else? Aha. Netflix. What do we have here? Clockstoppers. Hmm? This ought to do. It's great. Holy shit!! This is about magic something!* Not directly, but indirectly. *Perfect timing.* I love it. It's pure medicine for my discombobulated soul. I'm thoroughly entertained and delighted. Maybe it's really a crap movie, and I'm just too screwed up to tell the difference. I dunno. I don't care. Two hours zip by. I feel a lot better. So much better, in fact, I decide I'm not going to cancel that five o'clock whitewater kayaking lesson after all. *Oh boy. Stupid mistake. Great mistake. What was I thinking?*

Three p.m. After the movie, I have some time to kill before I leave for my kayaking lesson. I fritter an hour away doing two spontaneous strange things I never do: stare intently at a goldfinch and practice tai chi. Normally, I would find such endeavors about as interesting as eating driveway gravel, but in my expanded, wobbly, *magic something* state, I find both of these activities quite fascinating. I decide to stretch a bit, in anticipation of my kayaking lesson. I begin by doing back bends to limber up my lower back. Then I twist and stretch my upper arms and back. Then . . . I am doing tai chi movements I have *never ever* done before, like some Zen-Aikido-Kung fu master from outer space. It blows me away. *I'm* not doing it. My body is—as if it were the most natural thing in the world, as if I'd done these movements ten thousand times before. *Astounding*. I instantly discover that the tai chi movements have an incredible effect on my body and mind. The tai chi amplifies *magic something*. I become focused, still, extremely alert, and grounded. *Hearing*. My hearing becomes amplified. *Body*. My sense of balance and coordination sharpen to an Olympic gymnast knife edge. *Smell*. My sense of smell increases. *Vision*. My sense of sight increases—and that's when I discover . . . I am being watched.

Right out the window—there on the bird feeder—gold-finches. I am instantly fascinated—another living creature with consciousness, with awareness, same as me; and they are watching me. *It's okay*. I lock eyes with one of them. *Timid. Fearful. They know something. What do they know?* I slowly walk toward the window. *It's okay*. The bird I am staring at stares intently back at me between feedings. *What does it know? It knows . . . it knows . . . this moment! This immediate moment—at all times*. I stop before the window. *Birds are completely in the moment, completely here and now. The bird knows . . . magic something. Not directly. No . . .* I linger and stare. The birds are completely fine with my presence, even though I am a mere two feet away. I make no jerky movements. I keep my eyes locked onto theirs.

The birds know I am no danger. *Birds . . . animals? . . . animals know magic? . . . No, that's not right. Magic something is animal! It's an animal awakening. Magic something is the return of total animal nature, at one and at peace with the total environment.*

Four thirty p.m. After my encounters with goldfinches and tai chi, I embark on my whitewater kayaking adventure. Sometimes, I just don't know when to quit. I commit. Kayaking it is. It takes about half an hour to get to the section of river where my lesson takes place. I get out and gear up. I have my own helmet, shoes, and life vest. No paddle, kayak, or skirt yet. My instructor arrives. He's in his twenties (of course) and has the rest of my gear. *Oh boy.* Water levels are low, so we probably won't be doing much surfing or chute running. It'll be a boat flippin' and maneuverin' lesson. Not easy under normal circumstances. *Mistake.* Not easy at all in my state. He's a good-looking and affable guy—what you might expect of a young kayaking instructor. *This guy is gonna think I'm retarded.* Time stands still with all of our interaction. I'm incapable of rushing, hurrying, or processing lots of rapid-fire information. *Please repeat that.* I'm hot-fire-steel melting into experiencing just THIS moment and my brain's other functions have all but shut down. *Ohhhhh God.* We gear up and get into the water. I have to pee. *God damn it. I have to pee.* I tell the instructor. This is a drag because now I have to get out of the kayak. I do so slowly. And then like a dog, I jump into the water right in front of the instructor and pee—in my bathing suit—in the river. I'm in the moment and don't/can't process a care in the world. My instructor practically turns beet red with embarrassment. *Oh!? That was wrong?* I fumble for an excuse while I get back in the kayak. *Excuse. Come up with an excuse.* I tell the instructor I'm going through a very bad time with allergies, and it's taking a toll on my thinking. Sorry if I seem a little loopy. He doesn't mind at all. *Polite. Nice. Smart.* I suffer through some very uncomfortable training. One of the main problems with this outing is that I feel like my state is also very uncomfortable for the instructor—like he realizes something is up with me but can't put his finger on it, and it makes him uneasy. Maybe it implicates him and his orientation (known or unknown) to *magic something.* I don't know. It's awkward. I end the lesson short. He understands. We head in. I pay him, and we say goodbye. I'm lucky I didn't drown, knock my head, or get eaten by piranha. What was I thinking?

Seven thirty p.m. I'm an intense volcano of *magic something* now. I want to explode. I'm frustrated with this half-baked, half-assed, hazy experience. I want it to bloom and clear up, or leave. I can't stand it. I drive home in a state of urgency, intensity, and anger. It grows and grows. I arrive home and desperately begin seeking help. I call a few *magic something* teachers I know. No answer. I call Will Davis. No answer. I call another friend. He knows about *magic something* but is clueless with regards to my current state. It's like talking to a wall. He babbles on and on. I cut it short. *Ugh. WTF! What am I going to do?!*

Nine p.m. Finally, I take matters into my own hands and erupt into a shouting fit of rage. There's a map of the world in my reading room, and I shout at it. *What do you want from me world!? What do you want me to do!?* I roar and find a voice in me I'd never known. A lion voice. An animal voice. A being voice eons old; the voice of the world; the voice of the universe. *I AM HERE! YES! I AM HERE, AS A MAN! I AM A MAN! I AM HERE!* I rip off my clothes. *I AM A MAN!*

Energy and heat vibrate and pour out of my hands, lips, and

feet. I'm on fire. I explode with sweat, heat, and energy. The original conscious animal. The original conscious predator. *I AM!* Not separate or in denial of anything. *I AM!* Everything. The World. The Universe. *I AM!* Ancient. Eternal. Forever.

Nine thirty p.m. Here in this moment, for the first time in my life, I fully and completely embrace and accept *magic something*. I'm exhausted beyond belief. I'm dead on my feet. It takes me an hour or so to calm down. I eventually lie down and drift off to sleep.

Irritation

It's five thirty a.m. I'm up and writing on my laptop. It's dark out. Everyone is still asleep. I manage to do this until about seven fifteen when Jeremy plods in sleepy eyed and blows the morning routine bugle.

The morning routine comes and goes, and at eight thirty I'm off to do several audio/video installations. Today is all about irritation.

I leave the house with a sore throat, runny nose, and itchy eyes. (I'm coming down with a cold! Sorry, *magic something* does not make you immune to disease, sickness, or death.) As I make my way down the road, a whole host of other things begin to irritate me—simultaneously—and I slowly morph into a fuming, obscenity grumbling, grouch monster from hell. I notice that both my windshield wipers and left turn signal are broken. The sun is glaring in my eyes, and I forgot my sunglasses. There's a hole in my pants. There's a bottle of water rolling around, out of reach, on the floor of my car and making a big racket. I have the heat turned up too much, and it takes me fifteen minutes to notice. And, finally, before I entered the car this morning, I noticed that one of my advertising magnets was missing, which means only one thing—it blew off sometime ago, unbeknown to me. Yes, I am slightly irritated.

All of this leads to today's *magic something* lesson which answers an age-old question about individuals who have realized and attained *magic something:* How come they're still assholes? I personally have known quite a few *magic something* teachers who were bona fide assholes. It's a good question, but simultaneously a naïve one. It's a good question in that it shows some discrimination and intelligence, instead of just sheepishly accepting all behaviors from a teacher. It's a naïve question in that nine times out of ten, the person asking it is projecting an uninformed, largely ignorant, and myth-based behavioral expectation onto that teacher—i.e., that *magic something* teachers are benign, peaceful, holy, giving, humble, without an ego, perfect, etc.

Well—no surprise here—I think this expectation is a load of crap. I can be wholly described by *none* of the above: benign, peaceful, holy, giving, humble, without an ego, or perfect. Yet, clearly, here I am trumpeting my own *magic something*—aha got it—horn. How do I reconcile this? Ultimately, I can't. There is nothing I can say, do, or write that will ever totally convince you that I have found it; that I am done with the search; that I live with *magic something;* that I am all of these things, yet simultaneously can be an irritable asshole. That's the burden of those who are awake to and attempt to teach *magic something:* 90 percent of the time, we are teaching what *magic something* is not; 10 percent of the time, we are teaching what *magic something* is. There's a mountain of misinformation out there.

So when someone asks why that teacher is an asshole, my reply is this: Because *you* are; and because perhaps that's all the depth about yourself you've come to understand, that is what is reflected back to you. The glass constantly appears half empty.

Yes, some *magic something* teachers are indeed assholes; doesn't mean you have to like them. I'd be willing to bet that you could learn a hell of a lot from them, if you were willing to look beyond their ass-wholeness. If you are sincerely seeking *magic something*, risk getting insulted. It will serve you greatly.

I arrive at my customer's house in not the greatest of moods. Luckily, my job there is a small one, and I am in and out quickly. Of course, paradoxically, while I am there and during my inter-action with the customer, I nosedive deep into heightened *magic something*. The rest of the day unfolds in a pretty okay fashion. I drive to another customer's house and do some installation work for him. More deep *magic something*. Job done. I depart. It's about four thirty p.m.

On my way home, I ring my auto mechanic. He happily accommodates me with an appointment to bring my car in the next day. I also drop by the magnetic sign store. They too are helpful and offer to replace my lost sign at a discount. I'm happy. Good resolution. I can go home less a few minor irritations.

When I arrive home, Jeremy is having fun with the baby-sitter. I unpack a delivery of UPS boxes and play with Lilly, the dog, for a spell. The sitter leaves. It's six thirty. Elisabeth is cook-ing. I offer to give her some peace and quiet while she does so. I wangle Jeremy into a fishing jaunt at the nearby small pond. He obliges. I grab my fly-rod, outfitted with a small grey mosquito fly, built for catching bluegill. He puts on his adorably cute fish-ing hat and grabs his small pole. We walk out into the front yard. The neighborhood trees are turning amber, gold, and bright red: hues signaling the end of one thing and the beginning of another.

The moon is out and full, resting among a handful of clouds that speckle the blue evening sky. We cross the street, hand in hand, and meander down to the pond. There, in the twilight of the late October sunset, we go fishing, father and son, world at our fingertips, time suspended, possibilities endless, *magic something* thick in the air.

The Library

Five men entered a library, all of them seeking the truth. This was the largest library in the world, spanning five city blocks and towering fifty stories high. It contained every book ever written, by every culture in the world. Each man knew that his task would be daunting, but each was confident that he would find what he was looking for . . . the absolute truth.

After a day of perusing, the first man found one book and declared: "Aha, I have found the truth! It is in *this* book! How lucky am I! It could not be any simpler. I must let the world know of this discovery!"

His name was religion.

The second man found a small alcove, hidden in an obscure wing on the fifth floor, containing one hundred books. He took a month to read through the books. Upon finishing, he declared: "I have found the truth! It is in *these* books. The truth could not be any simpler. This discovery will surely benefit all of society!"

His name was politics.

The third man visited many floors and read more than one thousand books. It took him nearly four years to complete his task, but upon finishing, he announced: "I have spent four years in this library, and at last I have found the truth! It is in *these* books! It is not so simple that every man can understand it, but it is *indeed* the truth. This great discovery is for all of mankind!"

His name was science.

The fourth man spent ten years in the library. He visited nearly every floor and read more than ten thousand books. He spent many hours meticulously creating and recreating what he had learned from the books he read. At the end of ten years, he had amassed a very large collection of wonderful and original items. When he finally stepped out of the library he proclaimed: "I have at long last found the truth! It is in *these* books! Here is the proof!" He then unveiled his great collection.

His name was art.

The last man entered the library. He started on the first floor. He eventually worked his way through all fifty floors. It took him nearly his whole life, but he read *all* the books. Upon completion, he very quietly and peacefully exited through the front library doors. He was never heard from or seen again. One day, someone discovered a small piece of paper lying next to the very last book the man had read. On the paper was written: "There is no truth here. You are free."

This man had no name.

Eventually, in the search for *magic something,* you read all of the books in the library and walk out a free man. When this happens is anybody's guess. You can't predict it. You can't control it. You can't speed it up or slow it down. It just happens.

When it does happen, you will have encountered the seventh archetypal step—the last step on the great journey to freedom. It happened to me mid-morning, Saturday, September 27, 2010. As testament to the utter falsity of that tiresome myth and belief that one must be living under extraordinary circumstances or during extraordinary times to realize *magic something,* I did so slouched in my office work chair while surfing the Internet. Yep, pretty ordinary.

I didn't even recognize it as such right away. To me, it was just another circumstance of heightened *magic something* that I had been privy to, by this time, many times. It took a few days to sink in, but, finally, I realized that it was one of the most amazing discoveries of my entire life: I was no longer suffering. I was no longer suffering! I WAS NO LONGER SUFFERING! This was an extraordinary discovery. Suffering was the fundamental reason I had gotten involved with all this silly *magic something* business to begin with. I had been suffering, miserably so, for most of my adult life, and I wanted it to end—God damn it!—I wanted it to end. Then finally, after years of seeking and seeking and getting my head lodged farther and farther up my own ass, when it did end, I didn't even recognize it! What a complete joke. And that's *magic something*—unpredictable, wild, and delightful.

I wouldn't trade my great adventure for anything in this world. As a matter of fact, I would boldly say: It's why the world is here. Whether or not you decide to partake in the adventure is entirely up to you. Some of us can't *not* do it. I was one of those poor suckers.

There's a great old *magic something* saying (I've held it close to my heart for most of my adult life) that goes something like this: *Best not to step on the path. If you do step on the path, best to finish it.* Damn true statement. I could never have imagined that the mountain I set out to climb twenty-some years ago was this huge, this colossal, this mind-bogglingly big. And I could never have imagined that the view from the peak would be so damned beautifully ordinary. It's been a great ride; I'm glad it's over. I'm forever free of the library. And now yes, truly, I have no name. Perhaps this part of me continues on forever? The other part of me, however, does have a name—Jeff—and he's simply here, along for the ride until the day arrives when he dissolves back into the great river of life. Until then, he and I will just have to get along, but he knows and I know that the no-name part—the *magic something* part—is in charge, and that is a good thing . . .

Archetypal Step 7: The Heart of Magic Something

Saturday, September 7, 2010. It's nine a.m. Just did the whole morning routine with Jeremy and Elisabeth, and now, alas, I have a bit of office work to attend to. Not my usual Saturday fun, but I'm behind in paperwork and need to play catch-up. I walk down to my basement office and plop/slouch into my old, high-backed, black-leather office chair. Take a deep breath. Feel the bored/anxiety knot tighten in my stomach. *I really don't want to do this crap. Why am I doing this crap?* Open the mail. Junk. Junk. Bills. Bill pile. Junk. Catalog. *Sigh. Bored.* Clean my desk a little. Go through my paper quotes file. Just one. *I'm avoiding it. Open the damned file and do it and get it over with. I don't want to get it over with. Well then fuck it. What do you want to do?* Deep breath. *I dunno—anything except that quote. Okay. Screw the quote. Really? Yes. Screw the quote.* Sigh of relief. Relax a little. *Surf the Internet? Yes. Surf the Internet. Magic something sites? Yes, magic something sites.* Surf. Switch. Read. Surf. Read a little. Switch. *Been there. Done that.* Surf. Switch. *Yep, got it. Tedious. Getting bored. Same old . . . Hmmm? What's this? Small website. Probably nothin' here. Hmmm? Okay, I'll read that.* Read. *Yes.* Read. *Okay. Slow down.* Deep breath. Read. *Yes!* Read. *YES!* Read. *YES! YES!* Read. *Holy Shit! Damn, this is good. This is really, really good.* Read. Read. Read. Read. *Fuck, this is powerful. This is one juggernaut little essay. No, this is one of the best damn magic something essays I've ever read.* Read. Read. Read. Read. Read. Finish.

I fall into a dizzyingly deep state of *magic something.* The previous stress is totally gone. I still couldn't care less about the quote, but am so embalmed in *magic something* that I attend to it anyway and finish it in record time. After I finish the quote, I reread the essay and am blown away again—by its sheer, frank, raw, honest depth and veracity. Elisabeth calls me for something. I add the website to my "favorites." I walk upstairs.

The rest of the day is sublimed by *magic something.* I go to bed that night, wondering, but not really caring, if it will last . . .

Good and tired, I fall asleep, not realizing that I have finally arrived at a long-sought-after summit—called happiness.

Epilogue

It's six thirty a.m. Today will make a good epilogue, because this day is pretty indicative of my life with *magic something* beyond this journal: Nothing much great happens, and I'm okay with it.

Today's summary: Jeremy, Elisabeth, and I step through the morning routine—not much *magic something* going on. I leave for an audio/video consultation at a church. At the church, I find that *magic something* kicks into high gear, but, simultaneously, I'm irritated because I'm a little tired of these consultations. On my way home, I stop and fly-fish for about an hour in a local river. *Magic something* is subtle and undetectable while doing so. After fishing, I drop by Five Guys Burgers for a late lunch. I shift back into a perceptibly clear *magic something* when I bump into my mechanic during lunch. We have a nice casual talk. I drive home, drop out of heightened *magic something*, and do office work until about five p.m. At about six, Elisabeth, Jeremy, and I go to a friend's house-christening party in the countryside. The house hasn't been built yet. The party is outside around a large bonfire. It's nice. *Magic something* is more subdued during this time, and I'm feeling pretty normal. We drive home and go to bed.

Here's the report on my state of being beyond this chronicle: I don't live in a constant state of super-heightened *magic something*. I live in what I call the *Infinite Plain of Well-Being*, which contains both *magic something* and complete ordinariness. Sounds fancy, but it's not. It's just the constant grounded state of my ordinary life. The *Infinite Plain of Well-Being* feels, well, just like today—*day 21*—like the flow of a healthy, strong, steady river tumbling down from the mountains, meandering toward the sea. Sometimes calm. Sometimes turbulent. Sometimes boring. Sometimes exciting. Essentially, it feels just fine. Before I awakened to *magic something*, my default grounded state was an existential depression which manifested itself as basic life dissatisfaction, suffering, and unhappiness. Everything was definitely not fine. This is gone now. Thank god it's gone! I am free. The *Infinite Plain of Well-Being* manifests itself as a peaceful ordinariness, as *magic something*, as contentment, and as happiness—all swirling together and joining like tributaries flowing into a great river. I am that river now. I am that river.

I am that river now. I am that river.

Elephant, Monkey, and Butterfly and the Adventure of the Stinky Blanket

Once upon a time, there was a little boy, who every night loved to have his papa tell him a bedtime story. One of the stories his papa frequently told him was about the adventures of Elephant, Monkey, and Butterfly. The little boy loved these stories, as the adventures were always new, exciting, and, best of all, funny. Every night the boy's papa would make up a new story. The little boy didn't always understand the story (because his papa would sometimes make them too silly or too complicated), but that was okay—the little boy loved them anyway. It wasn't the actual stories that mattered. What mattered was that every night, the little boy went off to sleep nestled in a cocoon of warmth, safety, security, and love, with his papa right next to him. (Jeremy, my best little buddy, this one's for you . . . no matter *how* old you are. . . .)

One day, Elephant woke up terribly unhappy. This was very strange for Elephant because he was usually a jolly soul; not today, however. Today, he was unhappy, and he couldn't figure out why. He'd had plenty to eat recently. He wasn't sick. No one was angry with him. No one he knew had made him sad. Even

Hyena, who sometimes irritated him, hadn't upset him. All he knew was that his heart was heavy and something, from his head to his toes, just didn't feel right. He decided to ask for help from his friends Monkey and Butterfly.

"Monkey," he moped, "I'm unhappy, and I don't know why."

"Hmmm," said Monkey. "Let's go eat some breakfast with Butterfly. Maybe a little food will cheer you up."

"All right, I guess," said Elephant.

Monkey hopped up onto Elephant's shoulder, as he usually did, and the two strolled over to Butterfly's house. Butterfly was out tending his gardens of flowers when they arrived.

"Howdy, Butterfly," said Monkey. "Want to join us for breakfast?"

"Sure, give me minute," Butterfly replied. "I've got some pretty thick weeds today."

"Elephant's not feeling so well this morning," said Monkey.

"Really? What's wrong, Elephant?"

"I don't know," said Elephant. "I woke up in a terrible mood. I'm horribly unhappy, and I don't know why."

"Dear me," said Butterfly. "Here, try some of this." Butterfly handed Elephant a small bunch of flowers and leaves, which Elephant grabbed with his trunk and stuffed in his mouth.

"Thanks," said Elephant. "What's is it?"

"Something for an upset tummy. Feel any better?"

Elephant paused and thought and looked around, then he lifted up his right rear leg. "Nope," he said.

"Oh, well. Let's get some breakfast," said Butterfly, and he flew up to perch on Monkey's shoulder, as he usually did. The three of them meandered over to Giraffe's diner to get some breakfast.

"Howdy, Giraffe," said Monkey. "What's cookin'?"

"Usual," said Giraffe. "What can I get you boys?"

"Elephant's not feeling so well this morning," said Butterfly.

"I'm unhappy," interjected Elephant.

"Unhappy?" said Giraffe. "Well I've got a cure for that! It's called bacon, eggs, pancakes, ham, lettuce, peanuts, bananas, and coffee! How does that sound?"

"That sounds great!" said Monkey.

"Monkey!" yelled Butterfly. "That's for Elephant!"

"I'll have three please," said Elephant.

"I'll have a . . . banana," Monkey timidly said.

"I'll have a glass of orange juice," said Butterfly.

"Comin' right up," replied Giraffe.

"Ho-hum," Elephant sighed and moaned.

"Don't worry," said Butterfly, "you just need to get some food in your stomach. That'll cheer you right up."

A few minutes later, Giraffe came out of the kitchen with their food and plopped it down in front of them. Butterfly sipped his orange juice. Monkey nibbled his banana. They both sat, anxiously waiting for Elephant to finish his plate. There was a lot of food on elephant's plate. They waited. And they waited. And they waited some more, until elephant finally finished.

"Well?" said Butterfly.

"Well what?" replied Elephant.

"Are you happy NOW?!" blurted Monkey.

Elephant paused and thought and looked around, then he lifted up his left rear leg. "Nope," he said.

"Ohhhhh, man!" said Monkey.

"Hmm," said Butterfly. "You really are in a pickle, aren't you? What are we going to do with you?"

"I don't know," Elephant moped.

"Listen, I've got an idea," said Giraffe. "Doc Rabbit is sittin' right over there in the corner. Why don't you go ask him?"

"Excellent idea!" replied Butterfly. "What do you think, Elephant?"

Before Elephant could reply, Monkey and Butterfly dragged him over to Doc Rabbit's table and plopped him down.

Doc Rabbit looked up from his newspaper and coffee. "Hello, gents. What can I do for you?"

"I'm unhappy," said Elephant.

"You are?" said Doc.

"He's miserable," said Monkey.

"Well, you look healthy enough," said Doc. "I've got a few minutes. Let's see what we can do for you."

Then Doc, who happened to have his medical bag with him, took out a few strange-looking tools, a stethoscope, some pills, and a magnifying glass. He began poking and prodding poor Elephant. Elephant took it all in stride. After about ten minutes Doc put all his tools away.

"Take this," said Doc.

"What is it?" said Elephant.

"You're depressed," said Doc. "It's an antidepressant."

"Good job, Doc!" said Butterfly.

"Okay," moaned Elephant, and he swallowed the pill.

They all waited a few minutes. Monkey and Butterfly were bubbling over with anticipation.

"Well!?" said Monkey.

"Well what?" replied Elephant.

"Are you happy NOW?!" blurted out Butterfly.

Elephant paused and thought and looked around, then he lifted up his left front leg. "Nope," he said.

"Ohhhhhh!" said Monkey.

"Sorry," said Doc Rabbit. "Hmmm . . . only one thing left to do."

"What?" said Butterfly.

"What?" said Elephant.

"The mouse," said Doc.

They all gasped and their eyes got very wide.

"The mouse!" said Monkey. "The witch doctor, voodoo, black magic, priest mouse!? Are you crazy!?"

"Got any better ideas?" said Doc.

"Let's go," said Butterfly adamantly. "Is this okay with you, Elephant?"

"I don't care," Elephant sulked. "Sure."

"Thanks, Doc. Thanks, Giraffe!" said Butterfly.

Butterfly flew up to Monkey's shoulder, then Monkey hopped onto Elephant's shoulder, and off they went.

It took them about fifteen minutes to reach Mouse's place. Mouse, they knew of course, lived in a secluded little cave near the edge of the valley at the bottom of Big Mountain. Elephant, Monkey, and Butterfly had never been to Big Mountain or to Mouse's cave, but they had heard many strange stories about it—skeletons, potions, booby traps, bats, magic crystals, and things of that nature. So they were slightly disappointed when, after arriving at Mouse's place, they saw no cave, or skeletons, or potions, or booby traps anywhere in sight. As a matter of fact, Mouse lived in a quaint thatched-roof house, complete with little stone walkways and flowering morning-glory vines. There was nothing scary or strange about it at all. In the front yard, in a lawn chair, lounged Mouse, sunglasses over his eyes, apparently tanning himself in the sun.

Elephant, Monkey, and Butterfly walked up to him, but Mouse didn't move.

"Ahem," said Butterfly.

Monkey looked closer at Mouse. "I think he's asleep!" Monkey whispered.

Butterfly reached out his hand to shake Mouse, but was interrupted.

"I'm UNHAPPY!" bellowed Elephant.

"Oh dear me, dear me," said Mouse. "What?! Who goes there?" Mouse took off his sunglasses and looked around. "Good heavens, that was quick. I must have fallen asleep. Elephant, Monkey, and Butterfly, I've been expecting you."

"I'm unhappy," said Elephant again.

"Yes, I know all about it," replied Mouse.

Butterfly interjected, "How could you . . . ?"

Mouse looked at the three of them, hesitated, then spoke: "A mouse knows many things."

"Doc must have called you," said Butterfly.

"No, no, Doc didn't call," declared Mouse. He paused, then spoke again, "A mouse knows many things. That's all you need to know."

"Well then," said Monkey, who was feeling a little shy up to this point, "can you tell us what's wrong with Elephant?"

"Well of course I can't," said Mouse.

"What! What!?" said Butterfly and Monkey, simultaneously.

"That's up to Big Mountain and the stinky blanket."

"The stinky what?" said Monkey.

"Big Mountain?" said Butterfly.

"I'm UNHAPPY," moaned Elephant again.

"Yes," said Mouse, "there is only one cure for what ails you, my friend. You must take the stinky blanket to the top of Big Mountain and fly it."

"Do what?" exclaimed Butterfly.

"Fly a blanket? Where?" cried Monkey.

"And your friends must accompany you," said Mouse.

"Big Mountain!?" shrieked Monkey. "To the top of Big Mountain!? How will that make Elephant happy?"

"This," said Mouse, "is the *only* thing that will make Elephant happy. A mouse knows many things."

"Okay then. Let's go," said Elephant.

"Wa . . . wait a minute," said Butterfly. "How do we get there? What do you mean 'fly the stinky blanket'? Is this a joke?"

"It's not a joke," replied Mouse. "Here is the blanket." Mouse reached underneath his lawn chair and pulled out a very large, orange-, purple-, and blue-striped blanket.

"Elephant," Mouse said, "you will know what to do when the time comes to do it. Take this stinky blanket to the top of Big Mountain and ride it. Good luck." With that, right before their eyes, Mouse vanished.

Butterfly and Monkey were speechless. Elephant began walking in the direction that Mouse had indicated.

"That was very strange," said Butterfly.

Monkey picked up the blanket and held it to his nose, and took a big whiff. "It doesn't even stink!" said Monkey.

"That was very strange," said Butterfly again, and the two of them bounded off after Elephant.

"Where should we put the blanket?" said Monkey.

"I . . . don't know," stammered Butterfly "Just . . . just place it on Elephant's back."

Monkey hopped onto Elephant's shoulder and spread the

blanket out. To his surprise, the blanket draped perfectly over Elephant's large body.

"How's that?" said Monkey.

"Looks great to me," said Butterfly. "Elephant?"

"Fine," said Elephant. Elephant was still *very* unhappy.

"To the top of Big Mountain!" said Butterfly.

"I gotta pee!" said Monkey.

The entrance to Big Mountain trail was just ahead. After relieving himself, Monkey hopped back onto Elephant's shoulder, Butterfly flew up to Monkey's shoulder, and away they went.

The Big Mountain trail was just wide enough to accommodate a small mastodon with a primate and flying insect on its shoulder. Elephant, Monkey, and Butterfly liked the trail. Large green leaves draped over it, providing shade and beauty. Vines drooped down to the forest floor. Birds and insects twittered (with beaks, not phones) and buzzed. Enough sunlight shone through so that they could easily see where they were going. It wasn't frightening or difficult at all. And to think they had avoided Big Mountain all these years because everyone they spoke to said it was a dark and dangerous place.

"Are we there yet?" said Monkey.

"Monkey," Butterfly said, "Big Mountain is five thousand feet high. You know how long it's gonna take us to get to the top?"

"No," replied Monkey.

"All day," said Butterfly.

"How we gonna get back in the dark?" Monkey whimpered.

"I have no idea," said Butterfly.

"What are we gonna eat?" said Monkey.

"I have no idea," said Butterfly.

"Where—"

"Will you two pleeeease shut up," said Elephant.

"Sorry," said Monkey.

"Ugh," groaned Elephant.

After a short while, the three lapsed into a silent rhythm. Elephant didn't mind the walk and simply plodded along with Monkey and Butterfly perched on his shoulder. They were so light and Elephant was so strong, he hardly noticed them at all. A few hours passed. Monkey and Butterfly had fallen fast asleep. Elephant rounded a corner and there it was. He had heard it for a little while now: a wide, frothing river of rapids was tumbling down the mountain, cutting right across the mountain trail. It was impassable.

"Hey you two," said Elephant. "Wake up." He then bellowed and uncurled his long trunk.

"Ack! I didn't do it!" screamed Monkey.

"Oh, my!" said Butterfly.

"Yeah," said Elephant.

"Oh, look at that," Monkey moaned.

"What now?" said Elephant.

"Hmmm," said Butterfly, "there must be *some* way across."

"There is no way across, except on my back."

"Who said that!?" said Elephant.

"I did."

Elephant, Monkey, and Butterfly looked down, and there in the water was a very large green crocodile.

"There's no way to cross on this side, except on my back. There's a boat on the other side," said Crocodile.

"I can't fit on your back," said Elephant.

"You can't," said Crocodile, "but he can." Crocodile pointed to Monkey.

"How do we know we can trust you?" said Elephant.

"You don't know," said Crocodile, "but you have no choice."

"I don't trust you," said Elephant.

"I know you don't. That's the test," said Crocodile.

"The test?" said Elephant.

"What test?" said Butterfly.

"What? You three thought you could just stroll right on up to the top of Big Mountain, with the stinky blanket no less, and fly it, just like that?" said Crocodile. "There's always a test!"

"What do you know about the stinky blanket!?" said Monkey.

"A crocodile knows many things," said Crocodile.

"Hey!" said Butterfly. "Mouse said that!"

"Maybe we can swim," said Monkey.

"I don't think so," said Elephant. "I don't like you, Crocodile. I don't trust you, but you are right; we have no choice."

"Sometimes you gotta let it go, Elephant," said Crocodile.

"Hmmmmf," said Elephant. "Monkey, what do you think?"

"I'll do it," said Monkey, "I suppose . . ."

"And once he's across?" said Butterfly.

"He can float back over in the boat, then all three of you can use it to cross," said Crocodile.

"Crocodile, if this is some sort of trap or trick, I'm going to find you, and I'm going to stomp on you," said Elephant.

"I would expect nothing less," said Crocodile.

"Hmmmmf," said Elephant. "Monkey, be careful."

Monkey jumped down off Elephant and hopped onto Crocodile's back.

"See, not so bad," said Crocodile.

"Wish me luck that I'm not dinner," Monkey said sheepishly; then with a look of nervous apprehension in his eyes, he grabbed hold of Crocodile.

"You'll be okay," said Butterfly.

"He'd better be," said Elephant.

Crocodile took off across the wild river, Monkey clinging to his scaly back. Crocodile was very careful to swim high in the water, so Monkey could stay dry and safe. They slowly swam out of sight. The minutes passed (agonizingly slowly for Elephant), and soon it had been nearly half an hour.

"I can't stand this," said Elephant. "This is driving me crazy. Where are they? They shouldn't be taking this long! We never—"

"Look!" said Butterfly. "There!!"

Far off in the distance was a small flat raft with a sail.

"Is that him?" said Elephant.

"I think so," said Butterfly.

Slowly the raft came closer, and perched on top of the mast was a small primate.

"Monkey!" exclaimed Butterfly.

Elephant let out a huge sigh of relief and trumpeted. Monkey was now dancing and cavorting all over the raft. He slowly pulled into shore next to Elephant and Butterfly.

"Boy, am I glad to see you," said Elephant.

"Me too!" said Monkey.

"Any trouble with Crocodile?" said Butterfly.

"Nope," said Monkey. "I even fell in the water on the other side and thought for sure I was an appetizer, but nope, Crocodile was good to his word. He picked me up and got me to the raft, just like he said."

"Never trust a crocodile," said Elephant, "unless you have to."

"You guys ready?" said Monkey.

"Yep," said Elephant.

"Yep," said Butterfly.

Elephant and Butterfly boarded the raft, and the three set sail across the river. Monkey jumped back on to Elephant's shoulder, and Butterfly perched himself on Monkey's shoulder.

After a while, Monkey got a very strange look on his face and crinkled his nose. "You smell something?" said Monkey.

"I do . . ." said Butterfly. "What is that!?"

Monkey looked around, then he leaned down to the blanket covering Elephant. "It's the blanket! The blanket!" said Monkey.

"Hmm," said Butterfly. "How do ya like that?" Butterfly thought for a few minutes, then he spoke again: "Elephant, how do you feel?"

Elephant paused and thought and looked around, then he lifted up his right front leg.

"I feel . . . slightly better," grumbled Elephant.

"Isn't that strange," said Butterfly.

"Now that is a stinky blanket!" said Monkey.

The three sailed across the river to the far side. At a small pier, they tethered the raft and hopped back onto land. Big Mountain looked different on this side of the river. Gone was the verdant lushness of the jungle. A more rugged and rocky landscape took its place. They found the old worn trail again and continued their journey, onwards and upwards.

The sun rose to its zenith, high in the clear mountain air. It shone down upon the three travelers as they plodded along the dry rock- and dirt-strewn path. Elephant swung his big trunk back and forth, assisting the momentum of his large torso and legs as he walked. Monkey and Butterfly were sleepy eyed as they jostled upon Elephant's big back. It was almost high noon.

Monkey tapped Elephant's back as he usually did when he wanted to stop. Elephant stopped, then Monkey (along with Butterfly) hopped to the ground.

"I'm hungry," said Monkey.

"Me too," said Elephant.

"Me too." said Butterfly. "But we have no food."

"Hmmmmf," said Elephant.

"I'm hungry," said Monkey.

"You said that," said Butterfly. "What we need is a fruit tree."

"A fruit tree? Where would a fruit tree be in this place? What we need is a banana tree!" replied Monkey.

"A banana is a fruit, you baboon!" said Butterfly.

"Oh," said Monkey. "Yeah, a fruit tree!"

"There is only one fruit tree in these hills."

Elephant looked at Butterfly. Butterfly looked at Monkey.

"Who said that?" said Elephant.

"I did."

They all looked up, and there, perched high above them on a silvery old dead branch, was a magnificent-looking red-tailed hawk.

"There is only one fruit tree in these hills, and it is located across the great ravine over that ridge," said Hawk, as he pointed west.

"Is it a banana tree?" said Monkey.

"A fruit tree," said Hawk.

"Do hawks even eat fruit?" said Butterfly.

"Hmmmmf," said Elephant. "Butterfly is right. Hawks don't—"

"No, we don't," interrupted Hawk, "but trust me, a hawk knows many—"

"Things," said Elephant, Monkey, and Butterfly, all at once.

"Hmmmmf," said Elephant.

Then they all sat silently, awkwardly, staring at one another.

"Okay," said Monkey, "how is it that everyone on this mountain knows many things except us?"

"Suit yourself," said Hawk. Then he soared from the branch. In a split second, he was nearly out of sight but yelled back, "If you want something to eat, you'd better follow me."

Elephant, Monkey, and Butterfly sat and stared as Hawk flew out of sight.

"What do you think?" said Elephant.

"I'm hungry," moaned Monkey.

"Hmmmmf," said Elephant. "Let's go."

Monkey and Butterfly hopped on to Elephant's back, and they trotted off in the direction of Hawk, who was now soaring in circles slightly west of their position. It took them a few minutes to arrive; the ridge Hawk had pointed to was rocky and steep, and climbing it was not easy for Elephant. Elephant rounded a sharp bend and stepped up to what appeared to be the crest and—

"Aaaaack!" said Monkey.

"Wowwwwww," said Butterfly.

Elephant blew his trunk loudly, then reared back onto two legs and in one quick movement, spun around and back down from the crest. Monkey and Butterfly nearly tumbled off. Elephant regained his footing, then slowly crept up again. All three peered over the crest and viewed a ravine that dropped straight down nearly five hundred feet. Across the ravine, about twenty feet away, was another cliff edge.

"Ohhhh, my," said Butterfly.

"Hmmmmf, I hate heights," said Elephant.

"You hate heights, or you're afraid of heights?"

"What?" said Elephant and looked around.

"Because you're going to have to cross that ravine if you want food," said Hawk, who had landed on a large dead tree about thirty feet above them.

"Oh, you," said Elephant.

"That ravine?" said Monkey.

"I don't see the fruit tree," said Butterfly.

"Right. Where's the fruit tree?" said Monkey.

"The fruit tree is about a half mile beyond the other side. You can't see it from this vantage point," said Hawk.

"I hate heights," said Elephant, "and I hate edges."

"Hating them makes no sense," said Hawk. "You're afraid of them."

"What difference does it make?" said Elephant. "We can't cross that."

"Yes, you can," said Hawk.

"How do you propose we do that?" said Butterfly.

"That," said Hawk, "is for Elephant to decide."

"Hey wait a minute," said Monkey.

"I'm afraid of heights," said Elephant.

"I know you are," said Hawk.

"Is this another test?" said Monkey.

Hawk lifted off from the large dead tree and took flight. As he did so, the tree shifted slightly and leaned farther out over the ravine.

"Yes," said Hawk, and he flew out of sight.

"Hmmmmf," said Elephant.

"Ehhh, boy," said Butterfly.

"I'm hungry," said Monkey.

The three just sat there for a few minutes, saying nothing to one another. Elephant moaned a few times as he pondered the situation. The wind blew, which caused a dry whistle as it touched upon the edges of the deep, brown-stained ravine. The sky above them was clear and blue.

"I have an idea," said Monkey.

"How did you suddenly get so smart?" said Butterfly.

"I told you," said Monkey, "I'm hungry. See that tree up there?"

"Yes," said Butterfly.

"Uhhhh . . .yeah . . ." said Elephant.

"Push it over. It will fall across the ravine," said Monkey.

"Creating a bridge!" said Butterfly. "I like that idea."

"I don't," said Elephant.

"Why not?" said Butterfly.

"Because I'm the one who has to push the tree," said Elephant.

"Oh," said Butterfly.

"Yeah," said Monkey.

"And even if I do climb up there—All The Way Up There!— and push the stupid tree over, the chances of it falling and creating a bridge are slim to none," said Elephant.

"Agreed," said Butterfly.

"Yep," said Monkey.

"So!!" said Elephant.

"So, eh, what are you waiting for?" said Monkey.

"Hmmmmf!" said Elephant, bellowing a huge sound from his long trunk. "I hate tests, too!"

With that, Elephant very carefully and very slowly began to

climb the treacherous slope to reach the tree. His heart pounded. His brow dripped with sweat. A few times, his footing was less than secure, causing small boulders to tumble down the hill into the ravine. A long time elapsed before Elephant heard the rocks hit bottom. He didn't like this test at all. Several times, he had to stop and rest to let his nerves settle down. Elephant was truly afraid of heights, and he trembled like a frightened country mouse every time he looked down. But he kept going and going and slowly, ever so slowly, a small voice of confidence arose in him; a voice that encouraged him to take the next step; a voice that soothed his frayed nerves; a voice that convinced him that everything would be okay. Elephant wondered about this voice, but was too busy concentrating to take deeper heed. He just climbed.

Then, at last, he stood in front of the gigantic dead sage tree— the same one Hawk had landed on. There it leaned, barely clinging to the side of the mountain and dangling directly over the ravine. Elephant didn't stop to think about it. He just charged, and with the full force of his immense body, head butted the tree right off the mountain. He stopped inches short of falling himself. He watched as the tree tumbled through the air. It flipped end over end several times. And then—it happened quicker than he could believe or perceive. He blinked his eyes, trying to comprehend what he was seeing. The old sage tree had lodged itself in the ravine end to end, forming a perfect bridge. Monkey and Butterfly were already on it, jumping up and down with joy. He couldn't hear them. They were so far away, but he knew they were laughing and hollering. He'd done it. It felt good.

"Hmmmmf," he said to himself. "I still don't like tests."

Elephant descended a lot faster than he'd ascended. The trip down was much easier, due in no small part to that voice of confidence that had grown in his head. Shortly, he came upon Monkey and Butterfly, both of whom were seated on the root end of the old sage as it lay spanning the ravine.

"Not bad," said Monkey.

"Pretty good," said Butterfly.

"Yeah," said Elephant. "It was nothing."

"Nothing!!" said Butterfly. "That was the most awesomely spectacular thing I've ever seen you do!"

"Yahoooooooo!" said Monkey and Butterfly, simultaneously.

"Hurray for Elephant!!" they both shouted. "Hurray for Elephant!!"

Elephant smiled. "Let's eat," he said.

"Good idea," said Butterfly.

"Let's eat bananas!" said Monkey.

Without hesitating, Monkey jumped onto Elephant's back and Butterfly perched himself on Monkey's shoulder. Elephant stepped onto the tree.

"You got this?" said Butterfly.

"I'll be fine," said Elephant.

Slowly and deliberately, Elephant crossed the ravine on the old sage tree. He didn't look down. He gazed steadily ahead and, in no time at all, neared the other side and jumped off onto firm ground. There was a small path heading west of the ravine. Elephant got right on it and headed for the fruit tree.

"I smell something," said Monkey.

"Oh, my," said Butterfly, "that's terrible."

"What is it?" said Elephant.

"How are you feeling?" asked Butterfly.

"Hmmmmf?" said Elephant. "I hadn't really thought about

it." Elephant shook his left rear leg and paused. "But now that you mention it, I feel . . . a lot better."

"Ohhhhhh, gads!" said Monkey.

"What!?" said Elephant.

"It's the stinky blanket!" said Monkey.

"It's awful," said Butterfly.

"Isn't that strange," said Elephant.

"No, it's not," said Butterfly. "I get it now. The blanket is absorbing your unhappiness, and the more it absorbs, the stinkier it gets!"

"Hmmmmf," said Elephant.

"Peeee-yeeeew!" said Monkey.

Elephant then stopped and spoke: "Look at that."

"What?" said Monkey.

"That," said Elephant and nodded up to the top of a small hill.

There, nestled squarely on top of the hill, was the most magnificently strange fruit tree they had ever laid eyes upon. Magnificent, because of its immense size; strange, because of the fruit that grew over every square inch. Sprouting from every branch on the tree was not just one type of fruit but *every* fruit from every fruit tree that had ever existed: apples, bananas, pears, mangoes, lemons, oranges, limes, peaches, kiwis, grapefruit—the list went on and on and on. Some of the fruit Elephant, Monkey, and Butterfly had never even seen before. It was jaw-droppingly beautiful. It was the single most awe-inspiring fruit tree they had ever seen. Hawk had spoken the truth: It was a *fruit* tree. They walked right up to the tree . . . and they ate . . . and they ate . . . and they ate. It was like eating heaven itself. Finally, when they had gorged themselves to the limit of gorge-ability, they lay down beneath the great tree and sank into a good, long afternoon nap.

"Elephant," Monkey said, sleepy eyed as he drifted off.

"Yes, Monkey," replied Elephant.

"I'm not hungry anymore."

"Me, neither," said Elephant. "Me, neither."

And with that, all three friends fell fast asleep.

Time passed. The afternoon sun began its descent into the western horizon. Big Mountain shifted its gears and prepared for the evening liturgy. A gaggle of clouds rolled in and shrouded its peak. Wind whipped down its slopes. The temperature slowly dropped, and the leaves of the great fruit tree rustled with the change. Elephant awoke to a very strange sensation on his trunk. It was cold. It was wet. He opened his eyes. On his trunk had landed a single snowflake. Somewhere near the peak of Big Mountain, a snowstorm had begun.

"Wake up," said Elephant to Monkey and Butterfly.

Monkey stirred. Butterfly stretched his wings.

"What's happening?" said Butterfly "It's cold."

"Brrrrrr," said Monkey.

"Snowstorm," said Elephant.

"Snowstorm!?" said Monkey. "Where?"

"Up there," Elephant said, and pointed his trunk straight up the mountain.

"Ohhh," said Monkey. "Isn't that . . . ?"

"Where we're going," said Butterfly.

"Hmmmmf," said Elephant. "Let's go."

"Looks like f-u-u-u-n," said Monkey begrudgingly, and he hopped up on Elephant's shoulder. "Peeeeee-yeeeeeew," said Monkey, "and it smells like fun, too."

"Hmmmmf," said Elephant.

Elephant, Monkey, and Butterfly began the last leg of their trek. With no idea what the conditions would be like, they bravely walked straight up the mountain into the snowstorm. It took nearly two hours before they reached the worst part of the storm. Elephant slowed to a crawl as visibility dropped to near zero.

"This sucks," said Monkey.

"Quiet," said Butterfly. "Elephant is concentrating."

"Hmmmmf," said Elephant. "This does suck."

"Told ya so," said Monkey.

"Maybe we should look for shelter," said Butterfly.

"It would have to be a pretty big shelter," said Monkey.

"Hmmmmf," said Elephant. "This is different."

"What?" said Monkey.

"We're not going up any longer," said Elephant.

"It's flat," said Butterfly.

"And wide," said Elephant.

"Cool," said Monkey. "Maybe—"

Just as Monkey spoke, Elephant's front left leg crashed through a thin sheet of ice. Down he went, tripping forward, throwing Monkey and Butterfly into the air. Elephant caught himself with his massive trunk and front right leg, and let out a loud, powerful trumpet.

Monkey and Butterfly sailed through the air, landing twenty feet in front of Elephant. Elephant flailed and struggled against the very slippery ice edge around the hole he had created. His right front leg was barely clinging to the ice. Elephant trumpeted again.

"Stretch out your leg."

"What?!" said Elephant. "What good will that do?!"

Monkey and Butterfly looked confused as Elephant spoke.

"I said, stretch out your leg so I can grab it."

This time Elephant noticed that Monkey and Butterfly were not speaking. Both were standing with jaws dropped and eyes wide open. Monkey slowly lifted up his arm and pointed behind Elephant. Elephant understood, but because of his position, he couldn't turn around.

"Hmmmmf. Who goes there?" said Elephant.

"No time for that. Just lift up your leg."

"Which leg?" said Elephant.

"Do it!" shouted Butterfly.

"Your right rear leg. That ice won't hold you forever," said the voice behind Elephant.

"Hmmmmf," said Elephant, and he lifted his right rear leg about a foot off the ground. Whatever or whoever was behind Elephant grabbed his leg and, with one powerful yank, pulled Elephant back to safety. Elephant flailed a bit more before getting all four feet on solid ground.

"Didn't want to grab your tail. That might have hurt."

Elephant squinted through the snow to see who the stranger was. About five feet away, lying comfortably in the snow, was the largest snow leopard Elephant had ever seen. Actually, it was the *only* snow leopard Elephant had ever seen.

"You two stay put," said Snow Leopard to Monkey and Butterfly.

"Thank you," said Elephant.

"No problem," said Snow Leopard. "What brings an elephant, a monkey, and a butterfly all the way up here?" he asked.

"This," said Elephant, and he threw the stinky blanket on the ground in front of Snow Leopard. "I'm sure you know what this is."

"Uh, no . . . I don't," replied Snow Leopard.

"A test. Isn't this another test!?" said Elephant.

"No," said Snow Leopard, "*this* is an extremely unstable and dangerous ice field; you stepped through it and nearly fell to your death."

"Is this another test!?" shouted Monkey.

"Is it safe to come over?" shouted Butterfly.

Snow Leopard got up and walked down to the ice and sniffed. "You can come closer by about five feet. Wouldn't go any farther than that."

"What is this?" shouted Butterfly.

"It's an ice field," replied Snow Leopard. "You're lucky to be alive. Probably safe for you two to walk on, but it's definitely no place for a three-ton pachyderm."

"Two tons," said Elephant.

"My bad," said Snow Leopard, "and that blanket you just threw at me stinks terribly."

"Of course it does," said Elephant.

"Oh, is that the—" said Snow Leopard.

"Yes," said Elephant.

"That's the stinky blanket," said Monkey. "We're helping Elephant take it to the top of the mountain so—"

"So he can fly it," said Snow Leopard.

"You *do* know," said Elephant.

"I told you it was a test," said Monkey.

"Yes, I have heard of it," said Snow Leopard. "Hmmm . . . rarely does one see the stinky blanket."

"Rarely does one see a snow leopard," said Butterfly.

"Touché," said Snow Leopard. Then he spoke directly to Elephant. "You can't cross this ice field, but, from here, it's the only way to reach the summit."

"That won't do," said Elephant. "I have to take the stinky blanket to the top of the mountain!"

"Well," said Snow Leopard, "they"—he gestured toward Monkey and Butterfly—"can take the stinky blanket to the top, but you cannot. Trust me; I know this ice field well. It will not hold an Elephant."

"That's impossible," said Elephant. "There must be a way."

"Sorry," said Snow Leopard.

"Hmmmmf," said Elephant.

"Let's think about this," said Butterfly. "There's no other route?"

"No other route," said Snow Leopard.

"We can do it," said Butterfly.

"Do what?" said Monkey.

"Take the stinky blanket to the top of the mountain," said Butterfly.

"But . . ." said Monkey.

"That won't work," said Elephant. "I'm unhappy. The blanket is for me."

"We don't know that it won't work," said Butterfly. "Maybe it will work even if you stay here."

"Hmmmmf," said Elephant.

"Seems logical to me," said Snow Leopard. "But what do I know?"

"You're supposed to know many things!" said Monkey.

"Eh? Ooo-kaay," said Snow Leopard, "I know this: That ice field covers a rocky canyon that's about thirty feet deep. Below the ice are massive, craggy, pointy, sharp rocks. The size of the ice field is about two hundred feet across and five hundred feet wide. Even I, an agile snow leopard, would not cross it at this time of year. In the summer, maybe, when most of the ice has melted."

"We can't wait for summer!" said Elephant.

"We'll do it," said Monkey.

"But it's *my* stinky blanket," said Elephant.

"No other choice," said Butterfly.

Elephant crashed down on his rear hind legs in a sitting position, something he did only when he was extremely unhappy or agitated. "It's mine," he moped.

"I'm sorry, Elephant," said Butterfly. "Maybe it will work."

"Hmmmmf," said Elephant. "Here, take it!" Elephant grabbed the blanket with his trunk and threw it to Monkey and Butterfly. Monkey caught it in midair.

"We can do it," said Monkey. "We'll take it to the top."

"Whatever," moaned Elephant.

"If you'd like, I can wait here with you while your friends take it to the top," said Snow Leopard.

"Hmmmmf," said Elephant. "Fine."

"We'll be as fast as we can," said Butterfly.

"We'll be here," said Elephant.

"Sometimes, my friend," said Snow Leopard, "you must accept defeat."

"I accept it," said Elephant. "But I don't like it."

"Not worth your life," said Snow Leopard. "Good choice."

"Okay," said Butterfly. "We're off."

Butterfly and Monkey waved goodbye and took a few tentative steps across the ice field. Elephant watched them as they walked slowly away, feeling as unhappy and depressed as he had ever been. He took a deep breath and let the unhappiness consume his whole gigantic elephant being. Time passed. Then, the voice of confidence he had experienced at the cliff was suddenly back. How strange it was that in his worst moment, the voice had returned. It was clearer now. Elephant stood up on all four legs again, feeling slightly better.

Maybe they're right, he thought to himself. *It could work.* He walked over to the ice field edge and let out a huge, loud trumpet. He could still see his friends Monkey and Butterfly crossing the ice field. The trumpet he made was so loud, in fact, that it startled Monkey half to death. Monkey lost his footing on the ice, tripped, and went careening across the ice.

"Eeeeeeee!" Monkey squeeled.

"Oops," said Elephant.

Monkey lost his grip on the stinky blanket, and it went flying into the air. Slowly the blanket floated to the surface of the ice. Upon landing, the blanket did a very strange thing. Monkey, Elephant, and Butterfly all watched in amazement as the stinky blanket instantly froze. It was now a huge stiff square. They all stood and stared. Monkey walked up to it and touched it. His slight touch caused the blanket to slide several feet across the ice. Monkey followed it and repeated the touch, this time harder. The blanket spun around and slid a fair distance across the ice.

"I have an idea!" shouted Monkey. "I have an idea!"

"What would that be?" said Butterfly.

"Well," said Monkey, "it's simple physics really. The surface area of the blanket is now large enough and wide enough to evenly displace all our weight on the ice. Factor in the average thickness of the ice field, the distance to the other side, and the viscosity of the ice surface, and I think it means we can all safely slide across the ice field—on the frozen stinky blanket!"

"Did you just say 'viscosity'?" said Butterfly.

"Yes," said Monkey. "That's the resistance ratio—"

"Stop," said Butterfly, "I can't handle . . . ehhh, never mind. It's a good idea. Let's slide back to Elephant."

"Okay," said Monkey.

Monkey stepped onto the blanket. Butterfly flew to his shoulder. Monkey pushed slightly on the ice behind them and easily slid halfway across the ice toward Elephant. Elephant couldn't believe his eyes as he watched Monkey and Butterfly perform this trick.

They did it again and slid right up to Elephant.

"Impressive," said Snow Leopard.

"Get on," said Butterfly to Elephant. "Monkey's a genius."

"Hmmmmf," said Elephant. He looked at Snow Leopard and said, "Whatdya' think?"

"Worth a try, I'd say. Get on. I'll shove you off," said Snow Leopard.

Elephant carefully stepped onto the frozen stinky blanket and tip-toed to the center.

Monkey stood on the blanket next to Elephant. Butterfly rested on Monkey's shoulder.

"Okay," said Elephant. "Oh, and thanks again for saving my rump. I owe you one."

"Anytime," said Snow Leopard.

Snow Leopard reached down to the frozen stinky blanket and, with one powerful motion, heaved it forward. The frozen stinky blanket immediately careered across the ice field, safely carrying Elephant, Monkey, and Butterfly. They all waved good-bye to Snow Leopard.

"By the way," Butterfly shouted to Snow Leopard as they slid farther away, "how did you see us in that heavy snow?"

Elephant, Monkey, and Butterfly had slid too far away to hear Snow Leopard clearly now. They weren't positive, but they could have sworn that part of what he said sounded like "knows many things." The frozen stinky blanket kept sliding and seemed to be gathering momentum as they neared the far side of the ice field.

"Are we speeding up?" said Butterfly.

"I think so," said Elephant.

Suddenly their speed dramatically increased and the wind began rushing by.

"We're going down hiiiiiiiiilllllllllll!" Monkey shouted.

"Hang on!" said Elephant. "We're going to—"

Elephant was interrupted as the frozen stinky blanket slammed into a large snow bank on the edge of the ice field. All three flipped into the air and tumbled head over heels into a deep pile of snow. The frozen stinky blanket flipped into the snow bank as well.

". . . crash," said Elephant.

"Weally," said Monkey with a mouth full of snow. "Phhlucccccck! Crash?"

"It worked!" said Butterfly.

"It did," declared Elephant.

"Now what?" said Monkey.

"The peak," said Elephant. "Where's the stinky blanket?"

"Hmmm," said Butterfly. He flew into the air. "Over here!"

Elephant worked himself out of the snow and trudged over to where Butterfly had pointed. Monkey followed in his footsteps.

"Hmmmmf," said Elephant. He grabbed the now nearly thawed stinky blanket and threw it over his shoulder.

"Oh my gaaaaaaaawwwwwwwd," said Monkey. "I'm going to be sick."

"What?" said Butterfly.

"The stinky blanket," said Monkey. "It reeks."

Butterfly flew up to Elephant's shoulder.

"Ohhhhhhhewwhh," said Butterfly, as his face turned green. "That is disgusting! Elephant, how do you feel, eh, now?"

Elephant thought for a moment, and he jiggled his front left leg. "I feel pretty happy," he declared.

"I should hope so," said Butterfly, still green in the face.

"But not *completely* happy," said Elephant.

"Which way is the top?" said Monkey.

"I imagine that way." Elephant pointed his trunk up toward a rocky crag. "But I don't know."

"I can't see the peak," said Butterfly.

"High pressure cumulus cloud system," said Monkey.

"Monkey, will you stop that!" shouted Butterfly.

"Stop what!?" said Monkey.

"Being smart!" said Butterfly. "It's freaking me out."

"Maybe we should try it here," said Elephant.

"What? Flying the stinky blanket? Is this the top?" said Butterfly.

"I don't know," said Elephant, then he flung the stinky blanket from his back into the air with his trunk. It dropped immediately to the ground. Elephant picked it up again and threw it a second time. This time the blanket seemed to float for a second, then it fell again to the ground.

"I think the wind caught it that time," said Elephant.

"Ohhh, man!" said Monkey. "Come on. Let's head for that crag up there."

"Elephant goes alone."

"No, Butterfly," said Monkey, "Mouse said we all go."

"That wasn't me," said Butterfly.

"Huh?" said Monkey.

"I didn't say that," said Butterfly.

"I did."

Elephant, Monkey, and Butterfly looked toward the rocky crag. There, lounging on a small, green, moss-covered rock, was Mouse.

"Mouse!" cried Monkey. "What the—"

"Elephant goes alone," said Mouse for the second time. "This part is dangerous. You two wait here. Shouldn't take long."

"But . . ." said Monkey.

"Don't worry," said Mouse, "Elephant can take care of himself. Elephant, are you ready?"

"Uhhh . . . yes," said Elephant. "How did you get here?"

"Time's a-wastin'," said Mouse.

"You are full of surprises, Mouse," said Butterfly.

"Let me guess," said Monkey. "A mouse knows many things."

"Yep," said Mouse, "and so do you, apparently." Mouse laughed. "Big Mountain is good for everybody!" Then he laughed again.

"Well, I guess. Good luck, Elephant," said Butterfly.

"Thanks," said Elephant. Then Elephant thought for a minute as he looked at his friends. "Monkey, Butterfly, this is for you . . ." Elephant stood up on his hind legs and let out the loudest trumpet sound he could make from his trunk. The sound was deafening. It echoed across the ice field and Big Mountain. It sent shivers down Monkey's and Butterfly's spines. Elephant picked up the blanket and threw it over his shoulders. ". . . the two best friends anybody could ask for."

"Ready?" said Mouse.

"Hmmmmf," said Elephant.

"How you feelin'?" said Mouse, as Elephant strolled up the crag.

"Pretty good but not perfect," said Elephant.

"Let's work on that," said Mouse.

Before they went out of sight above the cloud-shrouded crag, Elephant turned to his friends again and waved a silent goodbye with his trunk. Monkey and Butterfly waved silently back. Both had tears in their eyes. They didn't really know if they'd ever see their friend, alive, again.

Slowly, Mouse and Elephant walked up the steep, rocky crag through the clouds. For a few minutes, Elephant could see nothing and had to trust that Mouse knew the way.

"This is dangerous," said Elephant.

"Oh, this isn't the dangerous part," said Mouse, "this is." Then Mouse disappeared as he took one final step up. Elephant followed. As he did so, Elephant emerged from the clouds into clear bright sunshine. Mouse was waiting. Just beyond Mouse, rising fifty feet above his head, was the glorious snowcapped peak of Big Mountain.

"Just a few more steps," declared Mouse, and he shot off for the peak.

Elephant followed. The path was strangely clear of snow and relatively easy to walk.

"What's so dangerous about this?" said Elephant.

"Up here!" said Mouse.

Elephant finally arrived. Upon taking his final step to the peak of Big Mountain, Elephant recoiled with fear and quivered as his front left foot dangled over a precipice that was thousands of feet deep. He quickly pulled his foot back and looked on in awe.

There were no clouds on this side of Big Mountain. He could see for miles, probably hundreds of miles, he thought to himself. He could see the vast range of mountains that Big Mountain was a part of. It was incredible. It was humbling. Elephant sat down on his hind legs and took it all in for a few minutes.

"What now?" he said.

"It's time," said Mouse. "Fly the stinky blanket."

"Okay," said Elephant, and he reached around to his back and pulled off the stinky blanket and held it into the air . . .

"What are you doing, you big oaf?" said Mouse. "That's not how you do it. Put it back over your shoulders."

"Eh, okay," said Elephant, and he did.

"Okay," said Mouse, "now jump."

Elephant looked at Mouse. "Jump? Are you kidding?"

"No, I'm not. Jump," said Mouse.

"B . . . b . . . but . . ." said Elephant.

Mouse smiled. "I see the stinky blanket has done its job. Let me explain a little." Mouse sat down next to Elephant. "Indeed, my friend, the stinky blanket is absorbing your unhappiness. When you met Crocodile, you had to give up control. When you met Hawk, you gave up your fear of heights and your doubt. When you met Snow Leopard, you gave up your selfish dreams. All these things were getting in the way of your happiness. Now, you must jump and give up who you think you are."

"B . . . b . . . but . . ." said Elephant.

"Are you happy, Elephant?" said Mouse. "Truly?"

Elephant thought for a moment. "No," he said, "but I'm an elephant. I can't—"

"Exactly," said Mouse. "You're *not* an elephant."

"I'm not an elephant!?" said Elephant. "Then . . . what am I?"

"The question is not what," said Mouse, "the question is who. Jump and find out."

"B . . . b . . . but . . ." said Elephant. " Okay then, who are you, Mouse?"

"That is a good question," said Mouse. "A mouse knows many things." Then, right before Elephant's eyes, Mouse transformed into a snow leopard, then into a hawk. He looked directly at Elephant, then leaped from the peak of Big Mountain and soared into the open air. "I am Big Mountain. I am all creatures. I am everything, and I am nothing—just like you."

Then Mouse vanished into the thin air.

Elephant sat for a very long time, contemplating his situation. Finally . . . he closed his eyes . . . he stood up . . . and he jumped.

Except—it didn't feel like he had just jumped. It felt more like he had hopped, then landed on his feet again. He was pretty sure he had jumped. He opened his eyes and looked down. There, beneath his feet, was the stinky blanket. Below the stinky blanket was ten thousand feet of air. He was flying! He was flying the stinky blanket! With this realization, he felt light as the air and vastly relieved. He breathed big gulps of air. He felt like he'd never felt before. He didn't feel like Elephant at all. As a matter of fact, he couldn't conceive of himself as anything. Mouse was right! He felt completely empty! But even this he didn't really care about. Because now one thing Elephant knew for sure—he was happy! He jiggled his front legs. He stomped his rear legs. He wagged his trunk. Then Elephant did something that Elephant had never done before: he danced . . . and he danced . . . and he danced. Elephant was Happy.

Monkey and Butterfly were getting very worried. It had been hours since Elephant had gone up the crag with Mouse. It was getting dark, and worse, it was getting colder. They both stood, teeth chattering, in the shadows beneath the crag on Big Mountain.

"Sh . . . should we go up af . . . after them?" said Monkey.

"No, let's wait. They'll be back," said Butterfly.

"I . . . it's c . . . c . . . cold," said Monkey.

"Not over here it's not."

"Wh . . . what?" said Monkey. "I . . . it's cold everywhere."

"Not over here. Want a ride?"

Monkey and Butterfly looked above them and there, to their utter amazement, was Elephant, floating in the air on the stinky blanket.

"Elephant!" cheered Monkey and Butterfly.

"You . . . you came back!" said Monkey.

"Of course I did," said Elephant.

"You're flying the stinky blanket!" said Butterfly.

"Yes, I am," said Elephant, and he floated down to his friends. They hopped on.

"What happened?" said Butterfly.

"Well, uh . . ." said Elephant, "let's just say, an elephant knows many things." Elephant smiled.

"And?" said Butterfly.

"And, what?" said Elephant.

"How do you feel!?" shouted Butterfly.

"Oh!" said Elephant. "I feel great! I mean . . . Monkey, Butterfly, thank you, thank you, thank you! Now, I am Happy!"

Then Elephant let out a loud trumpet from his trunk and danced. Monkey and Butterfly started laughing . . . and laughing

. . . and laughing. And soon all three were dancing and laughing as they rode the magnificent, flying stinky blanket off Big Mountain and back home. From that day on, Elephant's stinky blanket—never stank again.

The End

About the Author

J. Stewart Dixon is pretty much like you . . . married, kid, dog, two cats, job, mortgage. He's a believer and living proof that something more is attainable (and extraordinary) right in the midst of ordinary life. He lives in central Virginia with his family. When he's not working (he owns and operates an audio/video installation company), he can be found cavorting with the fish, bears, and bald eagles on the local rivers with a fly-rod in his hand.

J. Stewart Dixon has pursued magic something for most of his adult life. He's seen and been with just about every type of awakened spiritual teacher imaginable—famous ones with huge followings, unknown ones with small followings, good ones, not so good ones . . . the list goes on and on. His own true awakening process began in 2004 and completed itself in 2010.

J. Stewart Dixon has been a very creative individual for most of his life. He has a bachelor of science degree in audio engineering and music production from Syracuse University. He's written numerous plays and musicals and has two professionally produced music CDs. Writing is second nature to him; *21 Days* is his first book.

For more information and to experience
an entirely different side of author
J. Stewart Dixon
visit:
www.spiritualityforbadasses.com
Real Life. Real Awakening. Real Advice.

publishing

Made in the USA
Monee, IL
01 October 2021